Ebonics

NEW PERSPECTIVES ON LANGUAGE AND EDUCATION
Series Editor: Professor Viv Edwards, *University of Reading, Reading, Great Britain*
Series Advisor: Professor Allan Luke, *Nanyang Technological University, Singapore*

Two decades of research and development in language and literacy education have yielded a broad, multidisciplinary focus. Yet education systems face constant economic and technological change, with attendant issues of identity and power, community and culture. This series will feature critical and interpretive, disciplinary and multidisciplinary perspectives on teaching and learning, language and literacy in new times.

Recent Books in the Series
Distance Education and Languages: Evolution and Change
  Börje Holmberg, Monica Shelley and Cynthia White (eds)

Other Books of Interest
Beyond the Beginnings: Literacy Interventions for Upper Elementary English Language Learners
  Angela Carrasquillo, Stephen B. Kucer and Ruth Abrams
Bilingualism and Language Pedagogy
  Janina Brutt-Griffler and Manka Varghese (eds)
Continua of Biliteracy: An Ecological Framework for Educational Policy, Research, and Practice in Multilingual Settings
  Nancy H. Hornberger (ed.)
Language and Literacy Teaching for Indigenous Education: A Bilingual Approach
  Norbert Francis and Jon Reyhner
Language Learning and Teacher Education: A Sociocultural Approach
  Margaret R. Hawkins (ed.)
Language Strategies for Bilingual Families
  Suzanne Barron-Hauwaert
Language Minority Students in the Mainstream Classroom (2nd edn)
  Angela L. Carrasquillo and Vivian Rodríguez
Learners' Experiences of Immersion Education: Case Studies of French and Chinese
  Michèle de Courcy
Making Sense in Sign: A Lifeline for a Deaf Child
  Jenny Froude
Multilingual Classroom Ecologies
  Angela Creese and Peter Martin (eds)
A Parents' and Teachers' Guide to Bilingualism
  Colin Baker
Power, Prestige and Bilingualism: International Perspectives on Elite Bilingual Education
  Anne-Marie de Mejía
Understanding Deaf Culture: In Search of Deafhood
  Paddy Ladd

For more details of these or any other of our publications, please contact:
Multilingual Matters, Frankfurt Lodge, Clevedon Hall,
Victoria Road, Clevedon, BS21 7HH, England
http://www.multilingual-matters.com

NEW PERSPECTIVES ON LANGUAGE AND EDUCATION
Series Editor: Viv Edwards

Ebonics
The Urban Education Debate
Second Edition

Edited by

J. David Ramirez, Terrence G. Wiley,
Gerda de Klerk, Enid Lee and
Wayne E. Wright

MULTILINGUAL MATTERS LTD
Clevedon • Buffalo • Toronto

Library of Congress Cataloging in Publication Data
Ebonics: The Urban Education Debate. 2nd ed./Edited by J. David Ramirez ... [et al.].
New Perspectives on Language and Education
Includes bibliographical references and index.
1. African Americans–Education. 2. English language–Study and teaching–African
American students. 3. Black English. 4. Language and education–Social
aspects–United States. I. Ramirez, J. David. II. Series.
LC2778.L34E26 2005
427'.973'08996073–dc22   2004017325

British Library Cataloguing in Publication Data
A catalogue entry for this book is available from the British Library.

ISBN 1-85359-797-X (hbk)
ISBN 1-85359-796-1 (pbk)

Multilingual Matters Ltd
UK: Frankfurt Lodge, Clevedon Hall, Victoria Road, Clevedon BS21 7HH.
USA: UTP, 2250 Military Road, Tonawanda, NY 14150, USA.
Canada: UTP, 5201 Dufferin Street, North York, Ontario M3H 5T8, Canada.

Typeset by Datapage Ltd.
Printed and bound in Great Britain by the Cromwell Press Ltd.

Contents

Acknowledgements

We would like to thank the Center for Language Minority Education and Research (CLMER) at California State University, Long Beach, and its executive director, David Ramirez, for providing the initial funding to make possible the publication of this book.

We would like to acknowledge the valuable assistance of those who made it possible to include background material in this volume. We are grateful to the Center for Applied Linguistics (CAL) Washington DC, in particular Dr Carolyn Adger, for granting permission to reprint several of the documents in the second part of this volume. These are:

> *A Linguist Looks at the Ebonics Debate*, by Charles J. Fillmore;
> *Ebonics and Linguistic Science: Clarifying the Issues*, by Walt Wolfram;
> *Dialect Readers Revisited*, by John R. Rickford and Angela E. Rickford;
> CAL Media Statement on Ebonics.

We would like to thank the following people and organizations who granted permission to reprint some of the material in this volume:

> Charles J. Fillmore, Walt Wolfram, John R. Rickford and Angela E. Rickford;
> The journal, *The Black Scholar*, for granting permission to reprint Dr Geneva Smitherman's article, *Black Language and the Education of Black Children: One Mo Once*;
> The Teachers of English to Speakers of Other Languages (TESOL) for granting permission to reprint their *Policy Statement on African American Vernacular English*;
> The California Association for Bilingual Education (CABE) for granting permission to reprint their *Position Statement on Ebonics*.

Introduction

This collection of papers and documents serves as a comprehensive resource for all who wish to understand the distant and recent history of the Ebonics debate. The array of analyses, historical documents, and media articles in this book is meant to provide a reference for teachers, school administrators, academics, students, in short: all those whose work impacts the lives of Ebonics speakers in our public schools. The papers in this volume were written in response to the national controversy that erupted in the aftermath of a resolution on Ebonics by the Oakland Unified School District in California, in late 1996. That resolution affirmed the need to incorporate an explicit focus on Ebonics as a means to combat allegedly racist practices in the schooling of African American children.

The ensuing national debate reflected an *argument*, or *controversy*, about the status and role of *Ebonics*, a.k.a., *Black English*, *African American Vernacular English* (AAVE), *Black dialect*, or *African American Language* (AAL), in urban education. In recent years, this issue has not been debated much in public discourse, which raises the question: why now a book about a controversy that seemingly has died down completely? The answer is simple. Even though public attention to the issue of Ebonics ebbs and flows, the children who enter our public schools speaking Ebonics are there all the time, and in most cases, these children do not receive the type of education that adequately addresses their linguistic strengths and needs.

In addition, since the original debate over Ebonics, there has been a fundamental shift in educational language and assessment policies with strong implications for speakers of Ebonics. President George W. Bush's education reform bill, the No Child Left Behind Act (NCLB), was signed into law in January 2002. A central component of NCLB is annual testing in grades 3–8 and once in high school, with the expectation that by 2014, 100% of students will achieve passing scores on their state's high stakes test. Many states are also utilizing these tests as high school exit exams. Schools, districts, and states must disaggregate test score results into several subgroups of students, with a specific category for African American students. For each subgroup, schools and districts must set annual measurable achievement objectives indicating how much that subgroup's test scores will improve the following year. If any subgroup of students fails to make 'adequate yearly progress,' the federal government can deem the entire school as failing to make progress. If a school is deemed failing for two consecutive years or more, it is targeted for assistance from the state, but is also subjected to series of sanctions. Schools that fail to improve could ultimately be taken over by the state or even a private company. Thus, the stakes are very high for schools to raise the test scores of all students.

The high standards, disaggregated data, and specific subgroup for African American students may be considered positive aspects of NCLB. Schools which may have ignored the needs of their African American students will no longer be able to do so, lest they risk the entire school being deemed as failing. The Black–White test score gap has existed for a long time. Simply mandating that the gap go away by 2014 will not suffice. There is also the danger that many African American students who complete 12 years of schooling will nonetheless be denied a high school diploma because of difficulties passing the tests. Given this new context, more attention will be given to African American achievement. Issues of the mismatch between the students' home language and the Standard English of the tests will no doubt be raised again. The unique linguistic needs of many African American students are well documented within this volume and in other research (see Recommended Readings). In fact, it was low test scores of African American students on state tests written in Standard English which led Oakland Unified School District to adopt its Ebonics resolution in the first place (see Rickford, this volume). While NCLB makes some concessions for accommodations and special treatment for special education students and students classified as limited English proficient, no such concessions are made for the unique linguistic needs for speakers of Ebonics.

The title for this volume might have just as easily been something like: *Ebonics: The Continuing Debate*, or *Ebonics: The Debate Revisited*, because we have faced these issues before, and will no doubt encounter them again, unless politicians, pundits, teachers of our children, and the public at large come to understand what linguistics have long known, that is, language diversity is not only a fact of life, it is a product of the creative potential of the human intellect, that which some have hailed as the defining characteristic of our species.

This current volume is an updated, second edition to the edition published in 2000. After reviewing the on-going media coverage of Ebonics issues since the publication of the original edition, we believe that the Oakland controversy, which began in late 1996, continues to be a major point of reference for both those who continue to attack and ridicule Ebonics as well as for a number of scholars, including many of those who have contributed to this volume (see, for example, Baugh, 2000; Delpit & Dowdy, 2002; Rickford, 2000; Wolfram *et al.*, 1999).

Unfortunately, language diversity, like ethnicity, social class, religious affiliation, and so-called 'racial' diversity – and usually in conjunction with them, all too often, provides a convenient basis for marking differences among us. These differences then provide a means for positioning people as being either *superior* or *inferior*. Once these differences are labeled, social rewards, privileges, and penalties are easily justified by those who have the power to impose their own standards as if they were universal. These imposed standards come to be viewed as products validated on the purported basis of 'common sense' criteria.

It is tragic that, even as we have democratized access to public education over the past century, we continue to impose language standards and expectations on children, *at the point of their entry into the educational system*, which methodically privileges some children, while disadvantaging others. Under NCLB, annual testing reinforces the importance of meeting these language standards. All children enter school with knowledge of the language of their parents, homes, and communities. When we ignore the knowledge that some children bring in favor of the knowledge that others have, we impose a criterion that renders a socially constructed minority being *deficient*, *at risk*, *remedial*, *nonstandard*, or *failing*. No society, as linguistically and culturally as diverse as ours, which sincerely claims to advocate educational equity and equal opportunity through education, would condone the ascription of these labels to some of its children, unless it were tacitly disingenuous in its affirmation of these principles.

Part 1 of this collection is based primarily on scholarly responses to the Oakland Resolution in 1996. The contributions reflect key issues and themes that linguists and educators have encountered since the early stirrings of the Ebonics debate. Most contributors (see for example, Adger, Baugh, Kifano, Smith, and Smitherman) discuss the range of linguistic analyses of Ebonics. Other contributors (e.g. Smitherman, Rickford) convey to us a sense of the long history of this debate and depth and breadth of scholarly research associated with it. We also look at the impact of the education system on speakers of Ebonics (see Adger, Baugh, Kifano, Smith, and Rickford) and the tried and tested education strategies that provide a responsible, empirically grounded answer to the educational needs of Ebonics speaking children (see Adger, Baugh, Rickford, Kifano, and Smith).

Part 2 includes additional relevant documents and materials that accompanied the controversy over the Oakland School District policies of 1996. Some of these documents represented hasty political responses to the media hype that the resolution generated. Others represented the attempts of scholars and professional organizations to inform and temper the public debate. They represent one slice in time in the ongoing saga of the tension between community languages and their speakers and misguided attempts to eradicate them. Part 2 also includes a listing of media articles that appeared after 2000, which indicates the on-going relevance of the debate over Ebonics.

To the extent that we, as scholars and concerned educators, understand these issues, we admit that we have had only minimal effect in influencing public debates on issues of educational equity generally, and language-in-education specifically. Our negligible impact has not resulted from want of trying. Many among our contributors to this collection have devoted their careers to providing a scholarly, socially responsive basis for understanding the importance of language diversity as a major area of concern in promoting educational access and equity.

It is doubtful that the controversy over Ebonics that resulted from the initial Oakland School Board resolution will be the final chapter of reactive policies derived from misinformation and injurious attitudes concerning the educational needs of our children. Hopefully, this collection will help to better inform the next episode.

Terrence G. Wiley, Gerda de Klerk, and Wayne E. Wright for the editors, Tempe, 2003

References

Baugh, J. (2000) *Beyond Ebonics: Linguistic Pride and Racial Prejudice*. New York, Oxford: Oxford University Press.

Delpit, L. and Dowdy, J.K. (eds) (2002) *The Skin That We Speak: Thoughts on Language and Culture in the Classroom*. New York: New Press.

Rickford, J. (2000) *Spoken Soul: The Story of Black English*. New York, Chichester: John Wiley & Sons.

Wolfram, W., Adger, C.T. and Christian, D. (1999) *Dialects in Schools and Communities*. Mahwah, NJ: Erlbaum.

Part 1
Ebonics in the Urban
Education Debate

Ebonics: Background to the Policy Debate

TERRENCE G. WILEY

This chapter addresses the Ebonics debate within the broader context of language policy and alludes to a number of historical factors. In setting a context for the Ebonics controversy, examples will be shown regarding how governments and schools react to language diversity in other circumstances while attempting to locate it within the broader context of language policy options.

There are in the world today somewhere between 4000 and 5000 languages, and there are many varieties of language (Skutnabb-Kangas, 2000). Those varieties with higher status are called languages, and those with lesser status are usually called dialects. Sociolinguists usually focus on two major types of dialects – regional and social. From a linguistic perspective, there is no conclusive way to resolve the difference between what we consider languages and what we consider dialects. One way to avoid the issue is to refer to both as 'varieties' of language. For the purposes of this discussion, the more salient point is that most varieties of language spoken by students have not been elevated to the status of school languages. In this country languages and dialects are usually considered mutually intelligible forms of a related language. For the Chinese, however, 'dialects' need not be orally mutually intelligible. So there is no absolute consensus on the difference between languages and dialects. Nevertheless, most children around the world enter schools in which there is some difference between the language variety they speak and the language of the school. Quite often, the language of the school is mutually intelligible with the language of the home, but many times it is not. When language differences between the child's and the school's language is acknowledged, consideration of those differences needs to be reflected in instructional and educational policies and instructional plans. Failure to do so merely stigmatizes children as being *nonstandard* or *non-native*.

The choice of terms in referring to the language(s) or language varieties children bring from home to school is significant because the choice of terms ascribes a status to them. Despite the fact that *dialect* and *vernacular*, as linguists use them, are intended in a neutral or descriptive sense, in popular speech, *dialect* implies something less than standard that has a lower status. Expressions such as *language varieties* (Hudson's sociolinguistics, 1980) have been offered as preferable ways to talk about the subject. In this discussion, the terms 'Standard English' and 'school English' will be taken as roughly equivalent.

Normally, acquiring the language of home and community is not a problem. Children do this naturally and quite well in the interaction with their parents and local speech communities. There are far fewer languages that have been *standardized* as languages of literacy than are spoken. Moreover, there are far fewer languages that have been elevated to the status of school languages. The acquisition of literacy, however, does not always come as naturally. It can, however, be acquired naturally if it is a part of one's environment (Schieffelin & Cochran-Smith, 1984), if literacy is used in a meaningful way. Literacy becomes a problem, however, when the language variety of the home and school differ. Quite frequently, not only the variety of the school and home differ, but so too do the ways in which language is used, as well as the purposes for which it is used. Thus, many children who come to school will be disadvantaged by the perception that they are deficient unless it is recognized that differences are quite natural.

Unfortunately, because many educators view language varieties of the home and community as deficient, they do not believe that children should have a right to their own language (Smitherman, 1995). For those educators, the idea that a child who speaks a minority language or a vernacular should have a right to instruction in his or her language is seen as a novel, if not a heretical notion. However, it is not really a new concept. In 1953, the United Nations passed a resolution to that effect. Unfortunately, despite that resolution, the status of language rights around the world is very tenuous. The legal foundation for language rights is on a very shaky constitutional foundation (Wiley, 2002). When language rights are discussed, the notion tends to be interpreted as meaning something different from freedom of speech – as if freedom of expression was conditional on the use of English. Unfortunately, even though organizations like the UN have taken positions on language rights, all too frequently nations do not act on them because these resolutions are not binding (Skutnabb-Kangas, 2002).

Currently in the USA, the majority of people speak English. Nevertheless, there are about 46 million people, according to the 2000 U.S. Census, who speak other languages. However, results of the 1990 Census indicated that 98% of adults in the USA speak some kind of English at some level (Wiley, 1998). What is meant by 'some kind of English?' Consider several background issues. First, English speakers are the second largest language group in the world right now, and English is the world's principal second language. In the early days of the Republic, Noah Webster did his best to make American English different from British English and to eradicate social and regional dialects (Lepore, 2003). However, today, when one travel's around the USA or around the world in many countries, one finds many native speakers of English who sound and speak differently. There are many *Englishes*. If that word jumps out at you, do not be surprised because your spellchecker probably will not recognize it either unless you add it, even though there is even a periodical entitled the *Journal of World Englishes*, which is devoted to the study of the subject. Nevertheless, if one use the word 'Englishes' in a composition for a freshman English class, the transgression will usually get it circled with a red pen, unless there is considerable explanation for which one is using it.

The notion of *Standard* English raises some technical issues. There is considerable consensus on what most of the features of the standard are as prescribed by notions of correctness, particularly as these have been conventionalized in written English. However, in the USA, there is no English academy of experts as there is in some countries with the authority to define all of the characteristics of the standard. Authority is deferred to dictionary writers, prescriptive grammarians, or English teachers. However, even among these, there is no absolute consensus. When the so-called American English Standard is compared to the British, we quickly become aware of variations in spelling and pronunciation, as well as interpretations of minor points of grammar and punctuation. Just as there is more than one Standard English, so too there are many varieties of English – many Englishes. Despite their differences, these varieties are mutually intelligible. This flexibility of English has provided it with the power to spread around the world. English then is something elastic – elastic enough to expand around the world and reflect local, regional, and social characteristics. English is also elastic enough to be indigenized or bear the mark of contact with other important languages. In India, for example, one finds English and Hindi existing side-by-side with one being infused and enriched by the other in varying configurations of borrowing and mixing known as 'Hinglish.'

Thus, even as English has changed the world, the world has changed English. Historically, this has always been the case in the USA as well, where English, despite Weber's lament, has always had varieties, both regional and social. Even 'native' English speakers came speaking different Englishes, and, in contact with one another here, developed new varieties of the language.

The fact that 98% of the people in this country speak some kind of English at some level makes the USA one of the most monolingual nations in the world – not *the* most, but *one* of the most monolingual. Given that fact, why are so many people so worried about perceived threats to English? Why do they fear that somehow it will be over-whelmed by other languages when all the evidence that we have indicates that the opposite is the case? Generations of immigrants have come here and subsequently lost their languages (Veltman, 1983, 1988, 1999). Most states, including California, have long since passed statutes mandating English as the official language of instruction and have conferred official status on English. Given the unquestionable dominance of English as the language of the land and the high status accorded to it around the world, there is no rational basis to support the fear that it is in any danger of losing its dominance.

An equally paranoid concern is that 'Standard' English is somehow becoming contaminated by other regional and social varieties of English. Lippi-Green (1994, 1997) locates the basis for these concerns in what she calls the *Standard English ideology*. She defines it as 'a bias toward an abstracted, idealized, homogeneous spoken language which is imposed from above. . . which takes as its model the written language,' and which has as its goal the 'suppression of variation' (Lippi-Green, 1994: 166). Often with the best of intentions, schools are one of the primary propagators and defenders of this ideology (Wiley & Lukes, 1996). Norms for standard language are derived from written or 'literate' varieties of language rather than from oral varieties (see Milroy & Milroy, 1985; Wolfram & Fasold, 1974). Beliefs about the formal standard of language are based on a 'taught,' that is, school-based variety of language (Illich, 1979; Wright, 1980), which explains why children must go to school to *learn* their 'native' language. Because the school variety corresponds to the language of some people more than others, the choice of *whose* language variety is taken as the standard has the effect of advantaging some students while disadvantaging others at the point of entry, unless we take steps to recognize and accommodate the linguistic differences (cf. Heath, 1983).

Language diversity among students has always been a fact of life. However, over time so-called 'creolized' varieties of language have tended to de-creolize – that means they have moved more in the direction of the dominant school language. Certainly we have plenty of evidence that has happened, *except when people have been denied equal access to the standard due to segregation and unequal education.* Thus, if certain segments of the population are not learning the high status school variety of the language that is expected in schools, we have to look at the social, political, and the economic contexts and at educational language policies in order to try to determine why this is happening.

In order to assess various school and governmental policies toward language diversity, it is useful to locate them in a language policy framework. In Table 1, *promotion-oriented* policies refer to an active governmental agenda in which resources are allocated to furthering the official use of minority languages (Kloss, 1998). *Expediency-oriented* laws represent a weaker version of promotion laws as they are not intended to expand the use of minority languages, but are seen only as a means of accommodating them on a short-term basis (examples include: US Title VII bilingual education programs to accommodate perceived English deficiencies of speakers of languages other than English; accommodation for bilingual ballots and court interpretation). *Tolerance-oriented* policies are characterized by the noticeable absence of state intervention in the linguistic life of the language minority community. Maintenance of an ancestral language is contingent on the community having the desire and resources to support it. *Restriction-oriented* policies are those which make social, political, and economic benefits, rights, and opportunities conditional on knowing or using the dominant language (formal restrictive policies were passed during the World War I era and their effects persisted until the 1960s. However, since the 1980s there has been movement toward language restriction again).

When we refer to Table 1, it is useful to think in several dimensions about language policies. The *easy* policies to identify are *official* policies. Examples include California's Proposition 63, which declared English to be the state's official language. Other examples include school policies in which English has been declared the official language of instruction. More commonly in the USA, however, language diversity is responded to within an environment in which informal practices have the same, or sometimes even more, force than official policies. Schiffman (1996) has called such practices *implicit* and *covert* policies. Implicit policies are those which may not even consciously start out to be language policies, but in fact have the effect of policy. Covert policies, as the word would

Table 1 Language policy orientations

Governmental/state/ agency policy orientation toward language rights	*Policy characteristics*	*Implications for Ebonics speakers*
Promotion-oriented policies	The government/state/ agency allocate resources to support the official use of minority languages.	Ebonics has never been promoted as a language of instruction.
Expediency-oriented policies	A weaker version of promotion laws not intended to expand the use of minority language, but typically used only for short-term accommodations.	Some educational programs have sought to recognize Ebonics as a legitimate variety of language, contrast it with Standard English, and use it to bridge to Standard English.
Tolerance-oriented policies	Characterized by the noticeable absence of state *intervention* in the linguistic life of the language minority community.	There have been varying degrees of tolerance and intolerance toward Ebonics based on the sensitivity and knowledge of educators.
Restrictive-oriented policies	Legal prohibitions or curtailments on the use of minority languages; age requirements dictating when a child may study a minority/foreign language.	See 'Examples of Legislative Reaction' (Part 2).
Null policies	The significant absence of policies that recognize minority languages or language varieties.	Most education programs that do not recognize Ebonics fail to develop policies that would be more beneficial in (1) not stigmatizing its speakers, and (2) learning Standard English.

Table 1 (*Continued*)		
Governmental/state/ agency policy orientation toward language rights	*Policy characteristics*	*Implications for Ebonics speakers*
Repression-oriented policies	Active efforts to eradicate minority languages.	Historically, under slavery, people of African origin were not allowed to use their languages even as they were not allowed to acquire English literacy.

This table draws from and expands Kloss's schema (1977/1998; see also Macías & Wiley, 1998). The 'Null' and 'Repression-oriented' categories did not appear in Kloss's schema. Kloss also limited these categories to formal governmental/state policies; however, this schema can also be applied to institutional agencies and institutional contexts as well as to implicit/covert policies/practices.

imply, are a little more sinister. They are policies that seek to use language or literacy requirements as a means of barring someone from some kind of social, political, educational, or economic participation. Historically, for example, literacy requirements for voting and English literacy requirements for entry to the USA for immigrants have been used as gate-keeping mechanisms to exclude people on the basis of their race or ethnicity (see Leibowitz, 1969).

Historically, there has never been any real controversy over promoting English or Standard English. Although advocates of English-only policies frequently depict bilingual advocacy groups as being against the promotion of English, bilingual education policy in the USA has always attempted to advance English education by building on and developing literacy in home languages. Many bilingual education advocates support a policy of English Plus; that is, they support the promotion of English and another language. Based on the policy framework depicted in Table 1, bilingual education has been based on a policy of expediency or accommodation.

Similarly, African American educators and parents have sought to have their children learn Standard English. There has never been any attempt to promote Ebonics as the medium of instruction. What remains controversial, is whether Ebonics should be acknowledged as a legitimate variety of language and, thereby, used to accommodate instruction and the acquisition of Standard English, particularly in the lower grades.

In the late 1970s there was serious experimentation with *expediency* tools for African American children, which included the use of 'dialect' readers such as those used in the *Bridge* program (Simpkins *et al.*, 1977) that John Rickford refers to in his chapter.

From a legal standpoint, the most significant case related to Ebonics is *Martin Luther King Junior Elementary School vs. Ann Arbor Board of Education*. Geneva Smitherman, one of the key witnesses on behalf of the plaintiffs for that case, has written a book on the subject which is highly recommended (see Smitherman, 1981). Over the years a certain mythology has developed about the case. Several writers, including Baugh (1995) and Schiffman (1996) have discussed this. One myth is that the judge ordered Black English to be taught as a language of instruction. The other myth is that this was a landmark case. Both of these claims are false. First, the judge did not order Ebonics to be taught or promoted. From the perspective of the framework in Table 1, his decision was in the category of expediency. Regarding the second myth, that is, that it was a landmark decision, this too is false. Unlike the better known *Lao vs. Nichols* (1974) case, the *King* case was neither decided by, nor appealed to, the Supreme Court. Rather, it was decided only at the Federal District Court level. The school district which lost the decision chose not to appeal it. Thus, the impact of the decision was only relevant for school districts in states within that federal court's jurisdiction.

It is also important to know some of the background about the case. Essentially, the lawsuit was not initially brought entirely on the basis of language. The case involved three aspects. Plaintiffs argued that students were being discriminated against based on (a) their race, (b) their social class, and (c) their language. For the plaintiffs, language differences were seen as significant only in their association with race and class. However, the judge limited his focus to language differences. The fact that the judge limited the case in this way illustrates the way in which language is often used as a surrogate for more salient issues involving race and class in the USA. Consider how one often can get away with criticizing someone's language, allegedly for 'correctness,' 'appropriateness,' or 'accent.' In civil discourse, however, one cannot get away with criticizing someone's race or social class. Following the Oakland School District's Ebonics controversy and the attention it was accorded by the media, Ebonics jokes functioned as surrogates for more blatantly racist ones (Baugh, 1999). In the *King* case the judge did something that was very consistent with how issues of race and class are dealt with in US policy. He avoided them and simply dealt with language. This strategy is significant because the case was really about institutional problems or what is usually called institutional racism which involves a systemic failure to respond to the needs of children with minority status.

In summarizing issues on the King case, Geneva Smitherman (1981: 20) very eloquently said:

> The fate of black children as victims of miseducation continues to be the bottom line in the case. It behooves us to constantly remind ourselves of this fact. King began with a claim against the institutional mismanagement of the children from the Greenroad Housing Project. It ended with a claim against the institutional mismanagement of the language of the children. But language is a fundamental aspect of one's identity, and in that sense the children's language is them, is their momma's, and kinfolk, and community, and black culture, and the black experience made manifest in verbal form. Our argument and Judge Joiner's ruling was that it is the obligation of educational institutions to accept it as legitimate, given this dynamic cluster of complex forces and get on with the business of taking care and educating black children and youth.

Again, one of the problems with the *King* decision was that it had only minimal impact because it was not a landmark case, even though in the minds of many of us who read and write about it, it sometimes seems to take on that status. Nevertheless, the decision demonstrates the potential of expediency policies to remove the sole burden for acquiring academic English from the student. It can thus be seen as an attempt to get the schools to share the burden of helping language minority children acquire school English.

When the decision of the Oakland School Board to use Ebonics as a bridge to school English was being widely decried and ridiculed, what the press failed to focus on is the fact that the overwhelming majority of language minority children, including speakers of Ebonics, are being educated in Standard English. Nevertheless, many language minorities continue instructional practices that fail to recognize their linguistic differences. Referring again to the framework in Table 1, restrictive policies result in punishment and stigmatization which can result in students resisting instruction (see Ogbu, 1987). Where policies have not been overtly restrictive of children's use of home/community varieties of language, a null policy response, that is, the significant absence of policies of accommodation has offered little direction for teachers of language minority children. Thus, if language minority children are not succeeding in 'mainstream' educational practices, then the burden of proof lies not with innovative attempts at accommodation, such as those in Oakland, to find some expedient way to intervene on behalf of language minority children. Rather, the responsibility lies with educational policies which ignore and fail to accommodate their language differences.

Returning to Table 1, some language policies are restrictive. Some restrictive policies target languages other than English, and others target the use of Ebonics specifically, or 'nonstandard' languages more generally. We have examples of these among those bills currently being put forward at the state and federal levels. Significantly, some of the same people who are opposed to recognizing and accommodating speakers of Ebonics are also the same people who are backing the attack on bilingual education. Some anti-Ebonics proposals would make it illegal to use any federal monies for the purpose of teaching or using the language as a bridge to Standard English. By framing their attack in this way, Ebonics opponents rule out efforts at accommodation and expediency. Apparently, the intent of these proposals is to stop the promotion of Ebonics. In fact, however, the only district-level proposals that have been put forward thus far have been expediency proposals to help children bridge to school English. By opposing the use of expediency measures, these restrictive proposals take an extreme position and reduce the options available to educators. Moreover, by failing to acknowledge the legitimacy of Ebonics and other varieties of English, these restrictive proposals place the burden for bridging linguistic differences between the child and the school squarely on the child.

In addition to the serious problem of miseducation for speakers of Ebonics, there are other reasons why a better understanding of other varieties of English needs to be addressed in schools. Linguistic discrimination is often a surrogate for more racism and other forms of social prejudice. In this regard, Lippi-Green (1994, 1997) has done an important analysis of accent discrimination, and she has devised a practical framework to illustrate the need for a shared burden of responsibility for communication between speakers of Standard English and those who speak so-called accented English. Accent is one dimension of what a lot of the controversy over Ebonics is about right now. Lippi-Green notes that so-called 'accented' varieties of English can be seen either negatively or positively. When differences between accented varieties are perceived negatively, the communicative burden is placed on the speaker of the accented variety. When, however, it is viewed more positively, or at least more neutrally as being just different, then the burden for communication and acquisition of the standard is shared. Both the speakers of accented varieties and the standard variety must find ways to negotiate the differences. Baugh (1999) has done extensive work on the discriminatory impact of these judgments, which result in differential treatment and overt discrimination. Thus, the real communicative challenge between speakers of the 'standard' and speakers of 'accented' English is not to comprehend the other; rather, it is to overcome social judgments made on the basis of language.

In education this does not mean that we should ignore differences between Standard English and 'accented' varieties. To the contrary, it means that we must acknowledge that there are systematic linguistic differences between Ebonics and school English. These differences, however, are not significant enough to impose an educational barrier unless educators treat them as if they are a corrupted version of the standard. When educators treat them as such, then the message sent to the child deals with much more than communicative content. It sends a social message to the child that the way you speak and the way your mom speaks marks you as a socially inferior person. In this regard, imagine your own child, or a child that you might have one day, and how you do, or would, respond to that child as a language learner. Our young children would not be very successful language learners if we were to always treat them as imperfect speakers of our language. In fact, we acknowledge that they are imperfect speakers of our language, and we have all kinds of strategies to accommodate them because we want to encourage them to talk to us and like us. So why, then, do we ignore what we do quite naturally as parents when it comes to educating children who do not speak as we do? If our goal is to have children speak to us and communicate as we do, we certainly do not facilitate the process by putting them down. To the contrary, if we send the child a message that we do not like or respect his or her speech, we send a message that is miseducational.

After the Oakland School District's Ebonics controversy, one such restrictive measure passed the California State Assembly (AB 1206; see other examples of legislative responses in Part 2). If it had ultimately been signed into law, this measure would have prohibited schools from utilizing state funds or resources tied to bilingual education programs, for the recognition of, or instruction in, 'any dialect, idiom or language derived from English' as defined by the bill. Significantly, these criteria are very specific. They craftily avoid the question of whether or not Ebonics is a dialect, an idiom, or a language. This policy was designed to restrict teachers from acknowledging or accommodating the home language varieties of many of the state's language minority children. Again, note that the proposed policy did not use the word 'Ebonics,' but it certainly targeted Ebonics. Moreover, if a similar policy were implemented in Hawaii, it would have a similar restrictive effect on the majority of that state's children who are speakers of Hawaii Creole English.

One major problem with all such restrictive proposals is that they deny the history and the legacy of linguistic oppression that was imposed on the ancestors of today's speakers of Ebonics. They ignore the brutal policies that actually led to the creation of African American varieties of language. Those policies were not merely restrictive, they were more insidious; they were repressive. In fact, the very first language policies in our colonial history forbade, under the threat of the severest of punishments, African peoples from using their native tongues. Parents were not allowed to transmit their African languages to their children. In a defiant, but creative, response to that oppression, African American varieties of language were developed.

The next major repressive policy that targeted African Americans was initiated in colonial times and then carried forward until the end of the Civil War. These policies were called compulsory ignorance (or illiteracy) laws (see Weinberg, 1995). They were incorporated into the colonial slave codes and were adopted later in the southern states. These statutes made it illegal for enslaved Africans to learn to read in English, and made it illegal for any whites to assist them in the endeavor. Punishments were severe for any who were caught attempting to learn or teach. Given this legacy, it is particularly disturbing to look at books on language policy in the USA and find that most ignore this aspect of our history. The absence of discussion is even more extraordinary if we consider that African Americans have always accounted for a sizable portion of the national population. At the time of the first US Census in 1790, African Americans accounted for almost one out of every five people counted in that census. Obviously, there is a need for much more historical work and comparative analysis of these policies and their impact on African Americans.

Native Americans were also victims of these policies long before most European language minorities were on the receiving end. Starting in the 1880s, Native American children were taken away from their parents; that is, they were abducted and put in boarding schools. Sometimes they were mixed together with other Native children who did not speak their language to make it harder for them to preserve their own languages. If they were fortunate enough to be with other children who spoke their language and were caught speaking it, they were severely punished. Obviously, they did not learn to speak English very well under those circumstances; however, one word that they did learn was 'soap,' because it was used to wash out the mouths of those who persisted in speaking the tongues of their mothers and grandmothers (Weinberg, 1995; Wiley, 2000).

What can we learn from the history of the various language policy options as they have been applied to different language minority groups? The more we have studied what has actually been done, the more we find that the words of Woodson (1933/1990: 19) 50 years ago remain true. In his book, *The Miseducation of the Negro*, which came back into print a few years ago because it is still relevant, Woodson said:

> In the study of language and schools, pupils were made to scoff at the Negro dialect as some peculiar possession of the Negro which they should despise, rather than directed to study the background of this language as a broken down African tongue. In short, to understand their own linguistic history,... is certainly more important to them than the study of French or historical Spanish grammar.

We certainly would not deny language minority students the opportunity to study languages such as French or Spanish, but Woodson's point emphasizes that not to know or understand one's own language yet to study another is, of course, an act of deculturation. Deculturation results from those language policies that either unintentionally or intentionally erase one's ancestral and contemporary culture. Regardless of their intended purpose, they result in subordination through deculturation. Subordinating policies fail to recognize the linguistic differences that children have in school. Any constructivist educational theorist or child-centered practitioner can tell you that children learn by building on their prior knowledge. Children learn language by building on the language that they already have. Consequently, if we do not recognize the linguistic resources that children bring with them to school, they are likely to be perceived as being at risk. But we must ask why children who are only five years old should be at risk. From whom are they at risk? How did they become at risk? These are questions we need to consider when we hear such labels being applied to the children we are morally and legally obligated to educate.

References

Baugh, J. (1995) The law, linguistics and education: Educational reform for African American language minority students. *Linguistics and Education* 7, 87–105.

Baugh, J. (1999) *African American Language and Educational Malpractice: Out of the Mouths of Slaves*. Austin, TX: University of Texas Press.

Hudson, R.A. (1980) *Sociolinguistics*. Cambridge, UK: Cambridge University Press.

Illich, I. (1979) Vernacular values and education. *Teacher's College Record* 81 (1), 31–75.

Kloss, H. (1998) *The American Bilingual Tradition*. Washington, DC & McHenry IL: Center for Applied Linguistics and Delta Systems (originally published by Newbury House, Rowley, MA, 1977).

Leibowitz, A.H. (1969) English literacy: Legal sanction for discrimination. *Notre Dame Lawyer* 25 (1), 7–66.

Lepore, J. (2003) *A is for American: Letters and Other Characters in the Newly United States*. New York: Vintage Books.

Lippi-Green, R. (1994) Accent, standard language ideology, and discriminatory pretext in courts. *Language in Society* 23, 163–198.

Lippi-Green, R. (1997) *English with an Accent: Language, Ideology, and Discrimination in the United States*. London: Routledge.

Macías, R.E. and Wiley, T.G. (1998) Introduction. In H. Kloss (ed.) *The American Bilingual Tradition*. Washington, DC & McHenry IL: Center for Applied Linguistics and Delta Systems.

Milroy, J. and Milroy, L. (1985) *Authority in Language: Investigating Language Prescription and Standardization*. London: Routledge and Kegan Paul.

Ogbu, J. (1987) Opportunity structure, cultural boundaries, and literacy. In J.A. Langer (ed.) *Language, Literacy, and Culture: Issues of Society and Schooling*. Norwood, NJ: Ablex.

Schieffelin, B.B. and Cochran-Smith, M. (1984) Learning to read culturally: Literacy before schooling. In H. Goelman, A.A. Oberg and F. Smith (eds) *Awakening to Literacy* (pp. 3–23). Portsmouth, NH: Heinemann.

Schiffman, H.E. (1996) *Linguistic Culture and Language Policy*. London: Routledge.

Simpkins, G.C., Simpkins, G. and Holt, G. (1977) *Bridge. A Cross-cultural Reading Program*. Boston, MA: Houghton Mifflin.

Skutnabb-Kangas, T. (2002) Marvelous rights rhetoric and grim realities. *Journal of Language, Identity, and Education* 1 (3), 179–205.

Skutnabb-Kangas, T. (2000) *Linguistic genocide in education – or worldwide diversity and human rights?* Mahwah, MJ: Lawrence Erlbaum.

Smitherman, G. (1981) Introduction. In G. Smitherman (ed.) *Black English and the Education of Black Children and Youth: Proceedings of the National Invitational Symposium on the King decision* (pp. 11–31). Detroit, MI: Center for Black Studies, Wayne State.

Smitherman, G. (1995) Students' right to their own language: A retrospective. *English Journal* 84 (1).

Veltman, C. (1983) *Language Shift in the United States*. Berlin: Mouton.

Veltman, C. (1988) *The Future of the Spanish Language in the United States*. Washington, DC: Hispanic Policy Development Project.

Veltman, C. (1999) The American linguistic mosaic. In S. McKay and S.L. Wong (eds) *New Immigrants in the United States* (pp. 58–93). Cambridge: Cambridge University Press.

Weinberg, M. (1995) *A Chance to Learn: A History of Race and Education in the United States*. Long Beach, CA: California State University Press.

Wiley, T.G. (1998) World War I era English-only policies and the fate of German in North America. In T. Ricento and B. Burnaby (eds) *Language and Politics in the United States and Canada*. Mahwah, NJ: Lawrence Erlbaum.

Wiley, T.G. (2000) Continuity and change in the function of language ideologies in the United States. In T. Ricento (ed.) *Ideology, Politics, and Language Policies: Focus on English* (pp. 67–86). Amsterdam, Netherlands: John Benjamins.

Wiley, T.G. (2002) Accessing language rights in education: A brief history of the U.S. context. In J. Tollefson (ed.) *Language Policies in Education: Critical Readings* (pp. 39–64). Mahwah, NJ: Lawrence Erlbaum Associates.

Wiley, T.G. and Lukes, M. (1996) English-only and Standard English ideologies in the United States. *TESOL Quarterly* 30 (3), 511–535.

Wolfram, W. and Fasold, R.W. (1974) *The Study of Social Dialects in American English*. Englewood Cliffs, NJ: Prentice-Hall.

Woodson, C.G. (1990) *The Mis-education of the Negro*. Trenton, NJ: African World Press (originally published by Associated Publishers, Washington, DC, 1933).

Wright, E. (1980) School English and public policy. *College English* 42 (4), 327–342.

Using the Vernacular to Teach the Standard[1]

JOHN R. RICKFORD

Introduction

California Senate Bill 205, the so-called 'Education: Equality in English Instruction Act,' was introduced in early 1997. Had it been successful, this bill would have ended the Standard English Proficiency Program [SEP], which was specifically designed to improve the Standard English skills of speakers of Ebonics or African American Vernacular English (AAVE). This would have been a devastating blow, not only for schools in the Oakland area, but throughout the state.[2] Later, California Assembly Bill 36, which would have gutted bilingual education in California of a lot of its key features, failed to pass out of committee on April 23, 1997.[3] On February 23, 1997, California State Assemblywoman Diane Martinez successfully introduced Assembly Bill 1206, which 'prohibits school districts from utilizing, as part of a bilingual education program, state funds or resources for the purpose of recognition of, or instruction in, any dialect, idiom, or language derived from English.' This bill was clearly aimed at forestalling any attempt to use bilingual education funds for speakers of Ebonics or African American English, and it was eventually approved and signed into law. It is crucial to dispel the unnecessary defensiveness and fear about language diversity that this and similar legislation represent, and to work together for the good of all students in California and across the nation.

The title of this article, 'Using the vernacular to teach the standard,' requires some explanation. By *vernacular* I mean more generally 'the everyday [and informal] language spoken by a people as distinguished from the literary language' (*American Heritage Dictionary of the English Language*, 1992: 1984). More specifically I am thinking of vernacular dialects, 'which seem to be typified by the use of nonstandard forms' (Wolfram & Schilling-Estes, 1998: 13). By *standard*, and more specifically *Standard English*, I mean 'the variety normally used in writing, especially

18

printing; ... the variety associated with the education system ... the variety spoken by those who are often referred to as "educated people"' (Trudgill, 1999: 2–3). As Wolfram and Schilling-Estes (1998: 12) note, what linguists call standard or mainstream English is often referred to popularly (if ambiguously) as 'correct English' or 'proper English'. These two terms tend to be defined in a negative fashion by saying, 'if a person's speech is free of structures that can be identified as nonstandard [e.g. ain't for 'isn't'], then it is considered standard' (Wolfram & Schilling-Estes, 1998: 12).[4]

Most of what was written and said in the media after the Oakland Ebonics resolution of December 1996 represented a misapprehension of the nature of the problem the Oakland School Board faced and the nature of the solution it was proposing. Most writers and commentators emphasized the importance of children learning Standard English in this society. In response to this, the Oakland School Board might simply have replied, 'Yes, we agree. But what's next? How are we going to achieve that?'

How (Badly) Schools Have Failed to Educate African American Students

Oakland's original aim was to extend the Standard English Proficiency [SEP] program which had been in place since 1981 throughout the state. The goal of this program is to use the vernacular to teach the standard. That is a key point. I begin this article where Oakland began its discussion – with the fact of *massive educational failure within the African American community.* Existing methods throughout the country are not working. The insinuation of the many vocal critics of Oakland's Ebonics resolution was that Oakland's innovations were misplaced, and that the existing situation in Oakland and in the rest of America was 'just fine, thank you.' However, the fact remains that the status quo with respect to the teaching of African American children in American elementary, middle, and high schools is far from satisfactory. One of the tragedies of the media coverage of Ebonics is that it failed to recognize the issues that led Oakland to the exploration of Ebonics and other solutions in the first place.

The kinds of failures among African American students evident in the Oakland School District in late 1996 are well known; for example, the fact that these students, who comprised 53% of the school district population, represented 80% of all suspended students, and recorded the lowest grade point average of approximately a 'C-' (see http://www.west.net/

~ joyland/Oaktand.htm; see also http://www.geocities.com/Athens/ Forum/2522/). This problem is not unique to Oakland or California. It is a national problem.

Test scores from Palo Alto and East Palo Alto (Ravenswood School District) are compared in Figure 1. Palo Alto is located in the middle of Silicon Valley, and includes the children of professors, computer scientists, and other highly educated professionals. Palo Alto is home to some of the best public schools in the country. Figure 1 reveals that in 1990, 3rd grade Palo Alto students scored at the 96th percentile in reading on the California Assessment Program (CAP) exam; 6th graders scored at the 99th percentile. Thus, these students performed better than 99% of students in the state. In writing, Palo Alto students scored at about the 94th percentile in 3rd grade, and by the 6th grade, they scored at the 99th percentile.

Across the freeway from Palo Alto is the Ravenswood School District in East Palo Alto. As shown in Figure 1, in 1990 the primarily African American and Latino students in the Ravenswood School District in 3rd grade scored at the 16th percentile on the reading component of the CAP exam, and they fell to the 3rd percentile by 6th grade. Other statistics reveal that by the 8th grade, their reading scores dropped to the 2nd percentile. In writing, Ravenswood students that year scored at the 21st percentile in the 3rd grade, and by the 6th grade they fall to the 3rd percentile. As test results from preceding and successive years demonstrate, this is a regular pattern. Somehow, the Palo Alto Schools are able to build on the skills and talents their primarily White children bring to the school and *add value* to them, so that very rapidly kids are performing

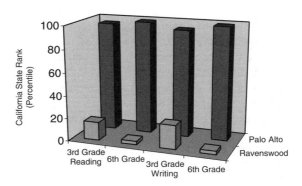

Figure 1 CAP test scores for Palo Alto and Ravenswood, 1990
Source: Peninsula Time Tribune, November 8, 1990, A2

at their maximum potential. Somehow, schools in East Palo Alto, with African American and other students of color, fail to do that, *subtracting value* instead. Students come in with a certain level of achievement and do steadily worse with each passing year. This is a forcible demonstration of the point Steele (1992: 68) made in his important *Atlantic Monthly* article on race and the schooling of Black Americans: 'The longer they [African American students] stay in school, the more they fall behind.'

That this is not merely a California phenomenon is revealed by recent data from predominantly African American schools in Philadelphia.[5] In the 1995–1996 school year, 41% of the students at Birney Elementary School were reading at the basic level or above as tested on the SAT-9; the school's overall reading score was 56.9. In the same district at Benjamin Franklin High School, however, the percentage of students reading at or above the basic level was only 7.6%, and the overall reading score was 24.4. The 1996–1997 statistics showed a similar downward spiral, although the extent of the drop between the elementary and high school levels was smaller. At Birney Elementary School, 34.4% of the students read at or above the basic level, and the school's overall reading score was 52.7; at Benjamin Franklin High School, only 14% of the students read at the basic level or above, and the school's overall reading score was 41.9.[6]

More comprehensively, Michael Casserly, Executive Director of the Council of Great City Schools, presented data before Senator Specter's US Senate Ebonics panel in January 1997 summarizing the performance of students in 50 large urban public school districts, including among them hundreds and hundreds of schools. Among other things, the data indicated that while White students in these schools show steady improvement in their reading achievement scores as they get older (60.7% read above the 50th percentile norm at the elementary school in 1992–1993, and 65.4% did so by high school), African American students showed a steady decline (31.3% read above the 50th percentile norm at the elementary school level, but only 26.6% did so by high school). Moreover, data from the 1994 National Assessment of Educational Progress, which he also presented, show the same depressing trend in a different way. On a 500-point scale, African American students at the age of nine are an average of 29 points behind the scores of their White counterparts; by the age of 13 they are 31 points behind; and by the age of 17, they are 37 points behind.

Thus, while the specific controversy surrounding the Oakland School District and their Ebonics resolutions engendered great debate, the educational malaise affecting African American students is general across the USA, particularly in urban areas. Moreover, the methods currently being used to teach reading and the language arts to African American students – with which the critics of Oakland's Ebonics solution seemed to be quite satisfied – are clearly not working.

Factors other than language, or even methods of teaching reading, are clearly involved in this kind of failure. Obviously, there are socio-economic and class issues and issues about the kinds of facilities which schools in primarily African American and White school districts tend to have. I was present at a meeting which the Rev. Jesse Jackson had with Board members of the Oakland Unified School District on December 30, 1996 (when he announced his revised position on their Ebonics resolution), and I was struck by his statement that the average US prison with large African American populations has better facilities than the average school with large African American populations. There is a frenzy of prison building, expansion, and renovation across the country as communities discover they are good business. There is not a similar frenzy of school building and improvement, thus we should not be surprised at declining levels of school performance.[7] And unfortunately, those who drop out of schools are more likely to end up in prisons or otherwise fall into the clutches of the criminal 'justice' system. As Jones (1995: 9) has noted, drawing on a 1995 report by the Sentencing Project, a national nonprofit organization, 'one in three Black men between the ages of 20 and 29 are within the grasp of the criminal justice system.'

There are also problems in terms of the kinds of teachers that most urban school districts are able to attract and the nonexistent or limited teacher training they have had (see Darling-Hammond, 2003). These problems are related to the fact that urban schools tend to pay lower salaries and have more challenging working conditions. And there are problems in terms of books and supplies. For example, my wife, Angela Rickford, a reading specialist, was doing a demonstration lesson on the teaching of reading recently at an urban school in the San Francisco Bay area. She asked the teacher for a storybook to read to the class. The teacher said, 'Storybook?' She didn't have any! The classroom lacked the shelves and tables of gaily colored and attention grabbing storybooks that are customary in suburban schools. Fortunately, one of the students in the classroom had a book in her backpack and that was used for the class demonstration.[8] Finally, teachers in schools with primarily African American and other ethnic 'minority' populations tend to have lower expectations for their students (Irvine, 1990: 54–61) and to ask less challenging questions. The evidence is overwhelming (see Tauber, 1996;

Rickford, A., 1998) that teacher expectations are closely tied to student achievement.

The Relevance of Ebonics

While factors like facilities, supplies, teacher pay and training, teacher expectations, parental involvement, and others are indisputably relevant, and while I would add my voice to those of others urging that these factors receive greater attention (see Comer, 1993, 1997; Cose, 1997; Irvine, 1990), I strongly dispute the claim of Ellis Cose in *Newsweek* (January 13, 1997: 80) that Ebonics – the language which many African Americans bring to school – is 'irrelevant.'

On theoretical grounds alone, we may assume that the language of African American students plays some role in the level of success they achieve in school, as language is so closely connected with cognitive abilities and with performance in other school subjects. Students who do well in English tend to do well in a variety of subjects across the curriculum; and those who do not do well in English, do not do well in most other subjects.

But there is empirical evidence that language may be related to achievement. For example, most students who fall behind in reading and otherwise fail in inner-city schools (see above) are from working class, rather than middle class families. The distinctive pronunciation and grammatical features of African American Vernacular English or Ebonics are used most commonly by members of the working and lower class. Table 1 summarizes data from Wolfram's (1969) study of Detroit.[9] Except for consonant cluster simplification and absence of plural -*s*, every other Ebonics feature in this table is far more frequent among the working class groups than among the middle class groups; for example, the lower working class uses multiple negation 78% of the time, while the upper middle class does so only 8% of the time.

The Detroit figures for working class Ebonics usage are not as vernacular as the data from East Palo Alto (Figure 1). In the latter community, recordings of working class teenagers (see Rickford, 1992) reveal copula absence figures of 81% and 90%, compared with the means of 57% and 37% in Wolfram's Detroit study, and with third singular present tense -*s* absence figures of 96% and 97%, compared with 71% and 57% in Wolfram's Detroit study. So, there is incontrovertibly a socio-economic class boundary which operates with respect to Ebonics usage.[10]

Moreover, the fact that working and lower class African American students tend to do worse in school than their middle class counterparts

Table 2 Use of selected AAVE features in Detroit, by social class (from Wolfram, 1969)

Feature	Lower working (%)	Upper working (%)	Lower middle (%)	Upper middle (%)
Consonant cluster simplification not in past tense	84	79	66	51
Voiceless *th* [θ] realized as → *f, t* or Ø	71	59	17	12
Multiple negation	78	55	12	8
Absence of copula/ auxiliary *is*, *are*	57	37	11	5
Absence of third person present tense *-s*	71	57	10	1
Absence of possessive *-s*	27	25	6	0
Absence of *-s*	6	4	1	0

may well be related to differences in their language use or to teachers' attitudes and responses to their language use.[11] The relevance of negative teacher attitudes to Ebonics was a key element in the 1979 ruling of Justice Joiner that the Ann Arbor, Michigan school district had failed to take adequate measures to overcome the barriers to equal education posed by the language of the African American children at Martin Luther King Jr. Elementary School (Labov, 1982; Smitherman, 1981). However, the evidence concerning negative teacher attitudes and responses to the vernacular of African American children had existed even earlier. Williams (1976) reported from a series of experiments that there were regular correlations between teachers' assessment of the relative 'standardness' and 'ethnicity' of students' speech and their ratings of the children's status and their confidence or eagerness: Students who sounded more nonstandard and/or non-White were also rated as being less promising or effective students. Williams and his associates also found in a separate experiment that prospective elementary teachers' perceptions of the relative standardness of children's speech were also affected by the children's race; 'the same sound track, when accompanying a videotape of an African American or Mexican American child, was rated as less standard than when accompanying a videotape of a White child' (Williams, 1976: 105). Thus, students of color experienced a double negative effect in terms of how teachers perceived and evaluated them in terms of race and language.

Piestrup's (1973) study of over 200 1st graders in predominantly African American classrooms in Oakland, California provides an even more powerful demonstration of the relevance and role of students' language – and how teachers respond to it. Piestrup found that there is a very strong inverse correlation between reading score and vernacular dialect score. The lower the dialect score, that is, the *less* students used the vernacular, the *higher* they scored on standardized tests of reading. This is interesting, but not unexpected, given what is known of the relationship between vernacular English usage and other factors like socioeconomic background which themselves correlate with school success. More interesting, but less well documented, is the relationship Piestrup found between children's reading scores and the different ways in which teachers *responded* to the vernacular in the classroom. In what Piestrup (1973: 131) called the 'Black Artful' style, teachers

> used rhythmic play in instruction and encouraged students to participate by listening to their responses ... attended to vocabulary differences and seemed to prevent structural conflict by teaching children to listen to standard English sound distinctions. Children taught with this approach participated enthusiastically with the teacher in learning to read.

By contrast, teachers using the 'Interrupting' approach 'asked children to repeat words that were pronounced in dialect many times and interpreted dialect pronunciations as reading errors. Teachers in this group presented standard English sounds for discrimination without ensuring accuracy of response' (p. 131). Some children taught by the Interrupting approach 'tediously worked alone at decoding without reading as if they understood; others seemed to guess at almost as many words as they were able to read. Some children withdrew from participation in reading, speaking softly, and as seldom as possible' (pp. 131–132). The latter result was not surprising, because each time they opened their mouths, the students were met with rebuke, reprimand, or correction.

Figure 2 shows more concretely the difference between these two approaches in terms of their correlations with dialect and reading scores. Note that children taught by the Black Artful teachers had higher reading scores overall than children taught by the Interrupting teachers. Moreover, the slopes for the two groups of teachers show that the students with the highest dialect scores (i.e. who spoke the most dialect), when taught by the Artful approach (line 5), read about as well as the kids with the lowest dialect scores (i.e. those who spoke the least dialect) when taught by the Interrupting approach (line 6). This is very clear evidence that the way in which teachers respond to and build on the vernacular can have a *powerful* effect on the level of success in reading which African American children attain.

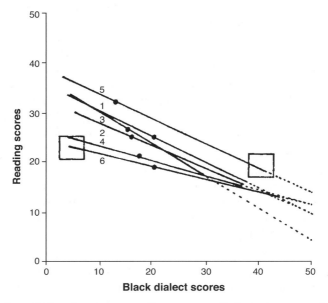

Figure 2 Correlation between reading scores, dialect scores, and teaching strategies, in Oakland 1st grade classrooms

(a) Higher numbers on the 'Reading Scores' axis indicate higher scores on tests of reading achievement. (b) Higher numbers on the 'Black Dialect Scores' axis indicate *more* vernacular dialect of AAVE usage and *less* standard or mainstream English usage. (c) 'Solid lines indicate the regression lines for actual scores; broken lines show the extension of these lines.' (Piestrup, 1973: 162). (d) 'Children with the highest dialect scores in Group 5 have reading scores approximately equivalent to children with the lowest dialect scores in Group 6. (Indicated by □ at the end of regression lines for Groups 5 and 6)' (p. 162).
Source: Piestrup (1973: 162)

Unfortunately, most teachers do not build artfully and skillfully on the vernacular. And most members of the public support them in this. In the debate surrounding the Ebonics controversy in December 1996 and the first few months of 1997, the predominant public response was, 'Stamp out Ebonics; or if you can't do that, ignore it, leave it alone, and hope and pray that it will go away. Bury your head in the sand; cover your ears with mufflers. Hear nothing. Don't let that virus anywhere near the classroom.' The undeniable fact, however, is that most African American children come to school fluent in the vernacular. It *will* emerge in the classroom, and *how* teachers respond to it can crucially affect how the students learn to read and how well they master Standard English. Ignoring or condemning the vernacular is not a particularly successful strategy, as shown in Piestrup's study, and as suggested by the massive educational failure associated with this approach nationwide.

The question may then be asked, 'How might the vernacular of African American children be taken into account in efforts to help them do better in schools?' I argue that there are three different approaches, as outlined below.

The Linguistically Informed Approach

The 'linguistically informed' approach encompasses the specific suggestions made by Labov (1995) based on decades of research on Ebonics or African American Vernacular English (AAVE). One of these is that teachers should 'distinguish between mistakes in reading and differences in pronunciation.' So AAVE speakers who read 'I missed him' as 'I miss him' should not automatically be assumed to have misread, in the sense of not being able to decode the letters. On the contrary, they may have decoded the meaning of this Standard English sentence correctly, but they may then have reproduced its meaning according to the pronunciation patterns of their dialect, in which a consonant cluster like [st] – the final sounds in 'missed' – is often simplified to [s]. Labov also suggests giving more attention to the ends of words, where AAVE pronunciation patterns have a greater modifying effect on Standard English words than they do at the beginnings of words. He also suggests that words be presented in contexts that preserve underlying forms, for instance, words that are followed by a vowel which favors retention of final consonants: *testing* or *test of*, rather than *test* in isolation. He also suggests using the full forms of auxiliary verbs (e.g. 'He *will* be here,' 'He *is* tall') and avoiding contractions (e.g. 'He*'ll* be here,' 'He*'s* tall'), because of evidence that once you go through a contraction stage, Ebonics is much more likely to proceed to deletion ('He Ø be here,' 'He Ø tall'). These are sound ideas that should not be controversial; but how much of an impact they will make on reading instruction for African American students is not yet clear, as no one has systematically implemented them or assessed their effects.

More recently, Labov and his colleagues at the University of Pennsylvania in collaboration with colleagues at other universities (including John Baugh and myself at Stanford), have begun an empirical study of the kinds of decoding errors which African American, Latino, and White elementary school students make in attempting to read. Their results are quite striking. Among other things, they report that the children almost never have trouble with single initial consonants (e.g. *b* in *bat*), but they have considerably more trouble with consonant blends and other complex initial consonants, with vowel nuclei, and with the codas or final consonants of words. The details (see Labov, 2001; Labov & Baker, 2003; Labov *et al.*, 1998) should prove useful to teachers as well as the designers of phonics textbooks.

Contrastive Analysis

The second approach is a form of contrastive analysis in which teachers draw students' attention specifically to the differences between the vernacular and the standard language.[12] One of the best examples of this is a study by Hanni Taylor (1989) at Aurora University. She was faced with a number of students from inner city Chicago who frequently used Ebonics features in their Standard English writing. She divided her students into two groups. With the control group, she used conventional techniques of teaching English and made no reference to the vernacular. But with the experimental group she used contrastive analysis, specifically drawing their attention to the points on which Ebonics and Standard English were different. What she found after 11 weeks (see Figure 3) was that the students who used traditional techniques showed an 8.5% *increase* in their use of Ebonics speech in their writing while the students who had benefited from contrastive analysis showed a 59% *decrease* in their use of Ebonics features in their writing. This is a very dramatic demonstration of the fact that, even if one agrees with the pundits across the country that students need to increase their mastery of Standard English, the contrastive analysis approach – essentially what Oakland wanted to do – is more likely to be successful than the conventional approaches that are currently being used. For example, one of the features that Taylor discussed was third person -*s* absence, as in

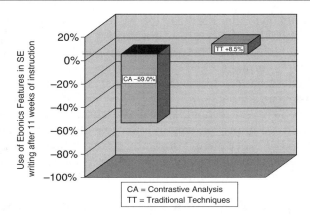

Figure 3 Effect of contrastive analysis versus traditional techniques among Aurora University undergraduates
Source: Constructed from data in Taylor (1991: 149)

'He walk Ø,' instead of 'He walks.' She found that students taught by traditional techniques did show a small reduction (− 11%) in the use of this feature over the course of 11 weeks, but the kids who were taught by contrastive analysis showed a massive decrease in the use of this feature (91.7%). Taylor found that overall this process of comparing the two varieties appears to lead to much greater metalinguistic awareness of similarities and differences between the vernacular and the standard and allows students to negotiate the line between the two much more effectively.

There are (at least) three other instances in which this approach has been successfully used to help Ebonics speakers improve in Standard English and reading. Schierloh (1991) reports a 30% improvement in the ability of 20 primarily African American adult dialect speakers in Cleveland, Ohio, to convert these sentences to Standard English after undergoing a two-week course in bidialectalism and contrastive analysis. Parker and Crist (1995) extol the virtues of the bidialectal contrastive analysis approach in teaching minorities to play the corporate language game. In this approach, teachers respect the home variety of the students and help them negotiate between that variety and the standard language, teaching them about appropriate contexts for different varieties of speech. The authors note they have used this approach successfully with vernacular speakers in Tennessee and Chicago at the preschool, elementary, high school, and college levels. There is also a program in

DeKalb County, Georgia, northeast of Atlanta. It was created by Kelli Harris-Wright, and involves use of contrastive analysis to help 5th and 6th grade students switch between home speech and school speech. According to Cummings (1997), the program 'has won a "Center of Excellence" designation from the National Council of Teachers of English. Last year, students who had taken the course had improved verbal scores at every school.' Harris-Wright also provides specific evidence of annual improvements in Iowa Test of Basic Skills test scores for students in her experimental program, compared with control groups of students in the DeKalb County school district. Thus, there is evidence from these programs that contrastive analysis works.

Introducing Reading in the Vernacular, Then Switching to the Standard

The final approach involves teaching students in the vernacular, introducing them to reading in the vernacular and then switching to the standard.[13] This follows a principle that was established from research conducted in the 1950s. Cheavens' (1957) dissertation on *Vernacular Languages in Education* is a classic work; it reported on studies around the world which showed that when students were taught in their vernacular or native language before switching to a second language which was not their vernacular, they tended to do better than direct instruction in the second language. One of the most dramatic examples was a major, in-depth longitudinal study conducted between 1948 and 1954 in 14 schools in Iloilo Province in the Philippines (see Orata, 1953). In this study, half of the students were taught completely in English for four grades while other students were first taught for two years in Hiligaynon, their native Philippine language, and then switched to English. What the researchers found is what other researchers have found in many other studies. Students who began in their own vernacular, when they switched to the second language, quickly caught up with the students who started in English, and even surpassed them. The students who started in the vernacular were outperforming – in English – the students who started in English in subjects ranging from reading to social studies, and even arithmetic.

The 'Bridge' study is the closest parallel to this in terms of the USA and Ebonics or African American English (Simpkins & Simpkins, 1981). This study involved 540 students, grades 7–12, in 27 different schools in five different areas of the USA. Four hundred and seventeen of the students were taught with an experimental series of 'Bridge' readers which began with narratives and exercises written in Ebonics. They then went through a transitional series of readers written in a variety intermediate between Ebonics and English, and ended with a final series written entirely in Standard English. A control group of 123 students was taught entirely in Standard English using conventional methods without the 'Bridge' readers. After four months of instruction and testing, the researchers found that the students who were being taught by the conventional methods showed only 1.6 months of reading gain (see Figure 4). This is consistent with the evidence presented earlier that the longer African American students stay in school with existing methods, the farther they fall behind. By contrast, the students taught with the Bridge readers showed 6.2 months of reading gain after four months of instruction. The experimental evidence was dramatically in support of the approach; the method offered the hope that African American students would finally be able to read above and ahead of the norm rather than below it. However, the inclusion of the vernacular in some of the 'Bridge' readers elicited knee-jerk negative reactions similar to those which emerged in the Oakland Ebonics debacle of 1996. The publisher of this innovative series of readers, embarrassed by the negative reactions, quickly decided against continuing production of the 'Bridge' series, and this very innovative and promising experiment came to an abrupt end despite its dramatically demonstrated pedagogical success.[14]

For many, this kind of information about the positive effects of taking the vernacular into account in education is probably brand new, even for those who followed media discussions of the Ebonics issue. This is due to the fact that 'the print media did little justice to the Ebonics story' (O'Neil, 1998: 43), and because of what Noam Chomsky has called more

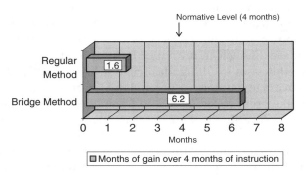

Figure 4 Reading gains using regular versus Bridge methods, Grades 7–12
Source: Constructed from data in Simpkins and Simpkins (1981: 238)

generally the 'manufacturing of consent' (see Achbar, 1994), the manipulation of information by the media to present certain sides of issues and exclude others. In keeping with Chomsky's insistence that 'the responsibility of intellectuals is to tell the truth and expose lies,' several linguists (including Geoffrey Pullum, Salikoko Mufwene, film-maker Gene Searchinger, and myself) submitted Op Ed articles on the Ebonics issue to major national newspapers such as the *New York Times*, *Washington Post*, and the *Los Angeles Times*. Our submissions were all declined. Some of us managed to get our points of view published in other sources (see Rickford, 1996, 1997c). However, it was an uphill struggle to get anything like a pro-Ebonics or provernacular perspective aired. Sometimes the newspapers would say, 'Well, the issue is passé.' However, the next weekend another editorial or Op Ed piece would appear ranting and raving about the horror that Ebonics represents or the wrongness of the Oakland resolutions. Thus, it was clear that it was not the timeliness of the issue that was in question, but the take on it which linguists represented.

Some Caribbean and European Parallels

Some brief parallels from the Caribbean and Europe suggest that ways of taking the vernacular into account, as described above, are not completely novel. I am originally from the Caribbean, and we speak varieties of Creole English there that are very similar to African American English in many respects; in fact I have argued in a number of publications (see Rickford 1977, 1986b, 1997a) that there is a historical relation between these varieties. In the 1950s, Robert Le Page, a well known British linguist, after going to Jamaica and noticing the appalling failures in the teaching of English and other subjects in the public schools, proposed that the first year or two should be taught in Creole before Standard English is introduced. A reporter from a local newspaper damned it as an insulting idea (cited in Cassidy 1970: 208); some of the press coverage on this issue in Jamaica from the 1950s sounds remarkably like press coverage of Ebonics in the 1990s in California. But as Le Page (1968) argued, there was a problem with the teaching of English across the 'English speaking' Caribbean: the percentage of students from each county who passed the 1962 GCE 'Ordinary' level exam in English was abysmally low, ranging from 10.7% to 23.1%. Le Page argued that there was systematic interference in the students' English from the Creole which was not being recognized by the teachers or the educational system, and that an approach that recognized and dealt with this interference would be more effective.

There was similar controversy in Trinidad in 1975 when a new English language curriculum that took Creole usage into effect was introduced (see Carrington & Borely, 1977). More recently, teachers working with West Indian students in North American schools have similarly felt the need to take their English Creole vernaculars into account; educators in Toronto have been particularly innovative in this respect (see Coelho, 1991), as have the developers of the Caribbean Academic Program for Caribbean English Creole speakers at Evanston Township High School in Illinois (see Fischer, 1992). For a more comprehensive review of attempts to take pidgin and Creole vernaculars into account in the education of their speakers, see Siegel (1999).

In terms of the European scene, two studies will be briefly described, although there are others that are relevant. The first is Österberg's (1961) study of Swedish dialects and education. Österberg conducted an experiment for a few years in which he began teaching one set of students in their vernacular dialect of Swedish and then switching to standard Swedish. A second set of students was taught entirely in standard Swedish for the same period. This was essentially a vernacular dialect version of research Cheavens (1957) had looked at earlier in terms of vernacular languages. Again, after 35 weeks, what Österberg found was that the dialect method showed itself superior, both in terms of reading quickly and rapidly assimilating new matter. The same positive results applied to reading and reading comprehension.

Between 1980 and 1982, Bull (1990) conducted a similar study in Norway, with ten classes of beginning students, encompassing nearly 200 students about seven years old. She used a design similar to Österberg's, comparing the progress of speakers of dialect varieties of Norwegian who were experimentally taught in their vernacular and then switched to instruction in standard Norwegian, with a control group schooled entirely in standard Norwegian. The results showed that the experimental dialect-instructed students read significantly faster and better than the control group of standard-instructed subjects; this was particularly true for the children who were performing poorly to begin with. Bull attributed this in part to factors similar to those described by Taylor (1989), that the explicit attention to the vernacular that the experimental students enjoyed made them better able to analyze their own speech and increased their metalinguistic awareness of language more than the traditional standard-based teaching methods.

Summary and Conclusion

To summarize, what led Oakland to its Ebonics resolution, and what has led many linguists (like myself) to get involved in this issue, is the depressingly poor record of American schools in helping African American students to read and write well and to succeed in school more generally. While other factors (e.g. teacher training, teacher expectations, and school facilities) are involved in this failure, the distinctive, systematic vernacular which many African American students speak (AAVE or Ebonics) is certainly relevant. Teachers, like many other people, often have negative and prejudicial attitudes toward the vernacular, and they do not realize that they can fruitfully build on it to help students master reading and writing in the standard variety (see Wheeler and Swords, forthcoming). One way of 'taking the vernacular into account' is to be more linguistically informed about the kinds of errors AAVE speakers make and the reasons for them, which opens up the possibilities for developing better strategies for helping students avoid or overcome these errors. A related approach, closer to what Oakland proposed, is to provide contrastive analysis between the vernacular and the standard to help AAVE speakers understand and bridge the differences, as has been tried successfully in Chicago, DeKalb County, Georgia and elsewhere. A third approach is to begin with reading materials and instruction in the vernacular and then transition to the standard, as has been tried successfully with the Bridge program in over two dozen classrooms in the USA and in similar programs with dialect speakers in Europe. Most people would be surprised to learn of the successes of methods of teaching the standard via the vernacular, the kind of approach the Oakland school board advocated; but this is partly because of their conditioned prejudices and because of the insidious manufacturing of consent and dissemination of misinformation and ignorance which the media effected on this issue, as on others.

In closing, I would like to turn on its head a comment that the Rev. Jesse Jackson made in his initial comment on the Ebonics issue, before he learned more about what Oakland was proposing and changed his mind. He was quoted in the *New York Times* of December 23, 1996 as saying that the kind of approach that Oakland was advocating represented 'an unconditional surrender, borderlining on disgrace.' I argue that to continue with traditional approaches in the light of their dramatic failure rates, and to ignore innovative methods of taking the vernacular into account despite their success and promise, represents an unconditional surrender, bordering on disgrace.

Notes

1. This is a revised and edited version of a paper presented at the California State University Long Beach Conference on Ebonics held on April 29, 1997. I am grateful to the organizers, including Robert Berdan and Gerda de Klerk, for inviting me to take part, and to Wayne E. Wright for helpful editing, and to Julie Sweetland for the Schierloh (1991) reference.

2. Fortunately, the bill was defeated in committee on April 2, 1997, although there have been subsequent attempts to resuscitate it in a significantly revised form. For further information on this and other California State or Assembly bills cited here, see http://www.sen.ca.gov/www/leginfo/SearchText.html, and consult Richardson (1998) for information on other legislative responses to the Ebonics controversy of 1996–1997 at the state and federal levels.

3. Proposition 227, the Ron Unz 'English for the Children' initiative, which essentially dismantles bilingual education in California, was approved in California's June 1998 primary election. Interestingly enough, only two ethnic groups voted (predominantly) against it: Latinos and African Americans. The percentage of 'yes' votes for the four major ethnic groups in California reveals how divided they are on educational and political issues: Whites 67%, Asians 57%, African Americans 48%, Latinos 37%.

4. The notion of standard or mainstream English is, of course, more complex and the subject of greater controversy than can be indicated here, involving considerations of social class and power which go beyond linguistic features. For more discussion, see Wolfram and Schilling-Estes (1998: 8–16), who distinguish between formal or prescriptive standard English, based more on writing and codified prescriptive grammars; and informal standard English, based more on spoken usage, sensitive to regional and social differences, and involving a continuum between standard and nonstandard usage. See also Lippi-Green (1997: 53–62) who assails the notion of standard language or English as an abstraction or myth in view of the considerable variation in usage and judgment which can be found both regionally and socially, even among 'educated' speakers. For various reasons, she prefers (building on Heath, 1983: 391–392) the term *mainstream* language. See also Bex and Watts (1999), which includes papers focusing more heavily on the notion of standard English in the UK, although some of them do consider US varieties too. The notion of 'vernacular' is less often discussed, but it is subject to ambiguity, too (Wolfram & Schilling-Estes, 1998).

5. These schools were deliberately picked to provide a comparison with data from the *Philadelphia Inquirer* of July 25, 1976 that were cited in Labov (1995).

6. One interesting aspect of the Philadelphia data for 1995–1996 and 1996–1997 is that the reading data from Cooke Middle School actually show an improvement over those from Birney Elementary School in terms of percentage reading at or above the basic level both years (47.5% and 40.1% respectively) although not in overall reading scores (53.1% and 51.2% respectively). This is somewhat encouraging as the 1976 data on reading and math combined which Labov (1995) cited show a steady and precipitous decline from the elementary level (31% of Birney students scored below the 16th percentile) through the middle school (50% of Cooke students scored

below the 16th percentile) to the high school (75% of Franklin students scored below the 16th percentile).

7. As Freccia and Lau (1996) note:

> In 1995, for the first time ever, California spent as much money on its prison system as it did on its universities. Since 1983, the California Department of Corrections has increased its staff by a huge 169%. . . By contrast, California has decreased its higher education staff by 8.7%. The California Assembly Ways and Means Initial Review of the 1994/1995 Budget states, 'Corrections spending has grown more than twice as fast as total state spending. . . this explosive growth has come at the expense of spending for other programs, primarily higher education.'

Given that African Americans are significantly over-represented in the jail and prison population – 'in 1991, African Americans constituted only 12.3% of the population nationwide, but 43.4% of the inmates in local jails, and 45.6% of the inmates in state prisons' (Rickford, 1997a: 173) – they are undoubtedly the primary 'beneficiaries' of the state's increased spending on prisons. But since spending on prisons comes at the expense of spending on schools, they are also the primary 'losers' in this process.

8. By contrast, I recently visited Los Angeles schools participating in the Language Development Program for African American Students, run by Noma LeMoine, and I was impressed by the ready availability of books in each classroom, many of them about African Americans.

9. Unfortunately, we don't have good large-scale class-based studies of vernacular usage in African American communities beyond the 1960s; it is an area in urgent need of empirical research. However, a small scale replication of Wolfram's study conducted in Oakland California by Stanford graduate student Catherine Chappell (1999) confirmed the sociolinguistic stratification and differentiation reported by Wolfram for Detroit three decades earlier.

10. The gap in Ebonics use between the working and middle class helps to explain the tremendous denial and condemnation evidenced by African Americans in 1996 and 1997 in relation to Ebonics. By and large, the people that the media interviewed were not from the African American working and under classes. Kweisi Mfume, Maya Angelou, Bill Cosby, *et al.*, were very much upper middle class 'representatives of the race,' and what they had to say about Ebonics was decidedly influenced by their backgrounds.

11. On this point, see Wolfram and Schilling-Estes (1998: 297–322).

12. The handbook of the standard English Proficiency [SEP] program for speakers of African American language, in use in California since the 1980s, and now used in varying forms in 300 plus schools, contains numerous examples of instructional strategies and drills for contrasting AAVE and standard English. See also Feigenbaum (1970) and Rickford (2001). Unfortunately, the SEP program has never been systematically evaluated on a statewide level (Yarborough & Flores, 1997), although plans are now afoot to implement such evaluation.

13. Note that this is *not* the approach that the Oakland School Board advocated in 1996.

14. McWhorter (1997) has pointed to a series of studies conducted in the early 1970s in which 'dialect readers were shown to have no effect whatsoever on African American students' reading scores.' I think it is important to re-examine and even replicate those studies, but it should be noted that they all differ from the 'Bridge' study insofar as they lacked any time depth. The studies cited by McWhorter were one-time studies of the effects of using vernacular or standard English stimuli on decoding or reading comprehension in the relatively brief (e.g. 30 minute) session or sessions needed to conduct the experiment, rather than studies of the effects of teaching children in the vernacular or in standard English over an extended period of time, as was the case with the 'Bridge' study. This crucial difference may account for the success of the latter study and the failures of the earlier studies. This much is suggested by the authors of one of the most comprehensive earlier studies, Simons and Johnson (1974: 355), who note that 'Another limitation of the present study concerns the length of the experiment and the number of reading texts employed. It may be the case that the treatment may have been too brief to show a difference in reading.'

References

Achbar, M. (ed.) (1994) *Manufacturing Consent: Noam Chomsky and the Media: The Companion Book to the Award-winning Film by Peter Wintonick and Mark Achbar*. Montreal; New York: Black Rose Books.

Bex, T. and Watts, R.J. (eds) (1999) *Standard English: The Widening Debate*. London: Routledge.

Bull, T. (1990) Teaching school beginners to read and write in the vernacular. In E.H. Jahr and O. Lorentz (eds) *Tromso Linguistics in the Eighties* (pp. 69–84). Oslo: Novus Press.

Carrington, L.D. and Borely, C.B. (1977) *The Language Arts Syllabus, 1975: Comment and Counter Comment*. St. Augustine, Trinidad: University of the West Indies.

Cassidy, E.G. (1970) Teaching standard English to speakers of Creole in Jamaica, West Indies. In J.E. Alatis (ed.) *Report of the 20th Annual Round Table Meeting on Linguistics and Language Studies: Linguistics and the Teaching of Standard English to Speakers of Other Languages or Dialects* (pp. 203–214). Washington, DC: Georgetown University Press.

Chappell, C. (1999) A generational study of Oakland AAVE: Linguistic variation by class and age among Oakland females. Ms. (qualifying paper), Linguistics Department, Stanford University.

Cheavens, S.E. (1957) *Vernacular languages and education.* PhD dissertation, University of Texas, Austin.

Coelho, E. (1991) *Caribbean Students in Canadian Schools, Book 2.* Markham, Ontario: Pippin Publishing and the Caribbean Student Resource Book Committee.

Comer, J.E. (1993) School power. implications of an intervention project (2nd edn). New York: Free Press.

Comer, J.E. (1997) *Waiting for a Miracle: Why Schools Can't Solve Our Problems, and How We Can.* New York: Dutton.

Cose, E. (1997) *Colorblind: Seeing Beyond Race in a Race-obsessed World.* New York: Harper Collins.

Cummings, D. (1997) A different approach to teaching language. *The Atlanta Constitution* January 9, B1.

Darling-Hammond, L. (2003) What happens to a dream deferred? The continuing quest for equal educational opportunity. In J.A. Banks (ed.) *Handbook of Research on Multicultural Education* (2nd edn) (pp. 607–630). New York: Macmillan.

Feigenbaum, I. (1970) The use of nonstandard English in teaching standard: Contrast and comparison. In R.W. Fasold and R.W. Shuy (eds) *Teaching English in the Inner City* (pp. 87–104). Washington, DC: Center for Applied Linguistics.

Fischer, K. (1992) Educating speakers of Caribbean English Creole in the United States. In J. Siegel (ed.) Pidgins, Creoles, and Nonstandard Dialects in Education (Occasional Paper #12) (pp. 99–123). Canberra: Applied Linguistics Association of Australia.

Freccia, N. and Lau, L. (1996) *Sending Kids to Jail: Progress in California Education.* On WWW at http://www.lifted.com/1.02/caleducation.html.

Heath, S.B. (1983) *Ways with Words. Language, Life, and Work in Communities and Classrooms.* Cambridge: Cambridge University Press.

Irvine, J.J. (1990) *Black Students and School Failure: Policies, Practices, and Prescriptions.* New York: Greenwood Press.

Jones, C. (1995) Crack and punishment: Is race the issue? *The New York Times* October 28, 1, 9.

Labov, W. (1982) Objectivity and commitment in linguistic science: The case of the Black English trial in Ann Arbor. *Language in Society* 11, 165–201.

Labov, W. (1995) Can reading failure be reversed? A linguistic approach to the question. In V. Gadsden and D. Wagner (eds) *Literacy among African American Youth* (pp. 39–68). Creskill, NJ: Hampton Press.

Labov, W. (2001). Applying our knowledge of African American English to the problem of raising reading levels in inner-city children. In S. Lanehart (ed.) *Sociocultural and Historic Contexts of African American English* (pp. 299–317). Amsterdam and Philadelphia: John Benjamins.

Labov, W. and Baker, B. (2003) What is a reading error? Unpublished manuscript.

Labov, W., Baker, B., Bullock, S., Ross, L. and Brown, M. (1998) *A graphemic–phonemic analysis of the reading errors of inner city children.* Manuscript, University of Pennsylvania. On WWW at http://www.ling.upenn.edu/~Labov/home.html.

Le Page, R.B. (1968) Problems to be faced in the use of English as a medium of education in four West Indian territories. In J.A. Fishman, C.A. Ferguson and J. Das Gupta (eds) *Language Problems of Developing Nations* (pp. 431–443). New York: John Wiley & Sons.

McWhorter, J. (1997) Wasting energy on an illusion: Six months later. *The Black Scholar* 27 (2), 2–5.

Orata, E.T. (1953) The Iloilo experiment in education through the vernacular. In UNESCO, *The Use of Vernacular Languages in Education* (pp. 123–131). Paris: UNESCO.

Österberg, T. (1961) *Bilingualism and the First School Language. An Educational Problem Illustrated by Results from a Swedish Dialect Area.* Umea: Vaster-bottens Tryckeri.

Parker, H.H. and Crist, M.I. (1995) *Teaching Minorities to Play the Corporate Language Game*. Columbia, SC: National Resource Center for the Freshman Year Experience and Students in Transition, University of South Carolina.

Piestrup, A.M. (1973) Black Dialect interference and accommodation of reading instruction in first grade. *Monographs of the Language Behavior Research Laboratory 4*. Berkeley: University of California.

Pullum, G.K. (1977) Language that dare not speak its name. *Nature* 386 (March 27), 321–322.

Richardson, E. (1998) The anti-Ebonics movement: 'Standard English-only.' *Journal of English Linguistics* 26 (2).

Rickford, J.R. (1977) The question of prior creolization in Black English. In A. Valdman (ed.) *Pidgin and Creole Linguistics* (pp. 190–221). Bloomington: Indiana University Press.

Rickford, J.R. (1986) Social contact and linguistic diffusion: Hiberno English and New World Black English. *Language* 62, 245–290.

Rickford, J.R. (1992) Grammatical variation and divergence in vernacular Black English. In M. Gerritsen and D. Stein (eds) *Internal and External Factors in Syntactic Change* (pp. 175–200). Berlin, New York: Mouton.

Rickford, J.R. (1996) Ebonics succeeds where traditional methods do not. *San Jose Mercury News* December 26, 8B.

Rickford, J.R. (1997a) Prior creolization of AAVE? Sociohistorical and textual evidence from the 17th and 18th centuries. *Journal of Sociolinguistics* 1 (3), 315–336.

Rickford, J.R. (1997b) Unequal partnership: Sociolinguistics and the African American speech community. *Language in Society* 26 (2), 161–197.

Rickford, J.R. (1997c) Suite for ebony and phonics. *Discover* 18 (12), 82–87.

Rickford, J.R. (2001) *Ebonics and education*: Lessons from the Caribbean, Europe and the USA. In C. Crawford (ed.) *Ebonics and Education* (pp. 263–284). London and New York: Sankofa World Publishers.

Schierloh, J.M. (1991) Teaching Standard English usage: A dialect-based approach. *Adult Learning* 2 (5), 20–22.

Siegel, J. (1999) Creole and minority dialects in education: An overview. *Journal of Multilingual and Multicultural Development* 20, 508–531.

Simons, H.D. and Johnson K.R. (1974) Black English syntax and reading interference. *Research in the Teaching of English* 8, 339–358.

Simpkins, G.A. and Simpkins, C. (1981) Cross cultural approach to curriculum development. In G. Smitherman (ed.) *Black English and the Education of Black Children and Youth: Proceedings of the National Invitational Symposium on the King Decision* (pp. 221–240). Detroit: Center for Black Studies, Wayne State University.

Smitherman, G. (ed.) (1981) *Black English and the Education of Black Children and Youth: Proceedings of the National Invitational Symposium on the King Decision* (pp. 11–36). Detroit: Center for Black Studies, Wayne State University.

Steele, C. (1992) Race and the schooling of Black Americans. *The Atlantic Monthly* April, 68–78.

Tauber, R.T. (1997) *Self-fulfilling Prophecy: A Practical Guide to its Use in Education*. Westport, CT: Praeger.

Taylor, H.U. (1989) *Standard English, Black English, and Bidialectalism*. New York: Peter Lang.

Trudgill, P. (in press) Standard English: What it isn't. In T. Bex and R.J. Watts (eds) *Standard English: The Widening Debate*. London: Routledge.

Wheeler, R. and Swords, R. (forthcoming) *In Their Own Words: Using Students' Vernacular to Teach Standard English in Urban Classrooms*. Urbana, IL: National Council of Teachers of English.

Williams, E. (1976) *Explorations of the Linguistic Attitudes of Teachers*. Rowley, MA: Newbury House.

Wolfram, W. (1969) *A Linguistic Description of Detroit Negro Speech*. Washington, DC: Center for Applied Linguistics.

Wolfram, W., Adger, C.T. and Christian, D. (1998) *Dialects in Schools and Communities*. Mahwah, NJ: Erlbaum.

Wolfram, W. and Schilling-Estes, N. (1998) *American English*. Oxford, UK: Blackwell.

Yarborough, S. and Flores, L. (1997, April 30) *Using Ebonics to Teach Standard English*. Long Beach Press Telegram.

Educational Implications of Ebonics

JOHN BAUGH

The Ebonics controversy and its educational implications cover broad subject areas, including anthropology, education, linguistics, sociology, and more. Some of the salient political issues are discussed in other papers in this volume. Each confirms the social significance of the Ebonics controversy, and there are several web sites that offer diverse opinions on the topic. Some of these efforts tend to trivialize the linguistic consequences of American slavery through editorial cartoons, and we find now that Ebonics, or at least the suffix '-bonics' has been integrated into the lexicon (e.g. suggesting that Jews speak 'Hebonics,' or that gay men speak 'Shebonics,' etc.). Bonics, and in this case '-ics' is a productive suffix in the English language. One editorial cartoon referred to 'Profanics,' combining 'profanity' with 'Ebonics,' thereby seeking to vilify the topic. As many people have interpreted Ebonics negatively, African American English has been castigated as linguistically erroneous; that is, as a corrupt form of English that is simultaneously vulgar and profane. However, when we look at the Ebonics controversy in its broader educational context, we see that the USA is somewhat unique with respect to the education of American slave descendants. We are one of the only advanced industrialized countries in the world that does not have a central ministry of education. Within this decentralized education, one finds a combination of public and private education in head-to-head competition. Public educators teach most African American students, and often do so with fewer resources than their private sector counterparts.

As a former British colony, the USA, once it gained national independence, adopted English as the primary national language, and then set about the task of how best to instruct students from various language backgrounds into English as a common linguistic denominator. Slave descendants differ, and differed, from all other

41

non-English-speaking immigrants because they were denied access to schools and literacy though laws that were intended to prevent Black literacy. And the Ebonics controversy alerts us to this unresolved racially designated paradox.

From an educational perspective, what are the best educational policies for the academic welfare of African American students and other students from low income and underprivileged backgrounds? Is Ebonics a separate language, or is it a dialect of English? What are the language qualities? There are incontrovertible political issues that are central to this as well: the dismantling of affirmative action, the Hopwood case in Texas, Proposition 209 in California, and debates regarding vouchers and school choice are all issues that politicians consider as they try to address issues of language. The Ebonics controversy has also accentuated issues pertaining to race relationships in the nation. However, there are competing professional definitions of Ebonics, to which we shall turn momentarily, but all of these things taken together compound the nature of the Ebonics debate.

The nation as a whole can be divided into three general linguistic categories: Category I includes native speakers of Standard English (SE), and here I want to take into account the national standard spoken by broadcasters like Tom Brokaw and Jane Paisley, as well as regional Standard English accents. For example, Senator Trent Lott of Mississippi speaks with a distinctive Southern accent, but he speaks with a standard Mississippi accent; Senator Ted Kennedy speaks with a Boston accent, albeit a standard Boston accent.

In Category II, we find speakers for whom Standard English is not native (i.e. SENN), and in Category III, are those for whom English is not native (i.e. ENN). These distinctions have been introduced in national studies of language minority students from across the country and their different linguistic backgrounds, and this brings me to you, the reader's, personal sociolinguistic profile.

Everyone who reads this text has a unique linguistic history, deriving from one of the three linguistic categories previously described, and I believe your own 'sociolinguistic relativity' may influence how you view this topic. Had you been educated in Texas, no matter what your linguistic background, you would be provided with the same instructional materials because they have a firm policy of statewide textbook adoption. All first graders get the same books, all second graders receive the same books, and all biology classes use the same books, etc. (i.e. within public schools). That procedure does not take linguistic diversity into account. A more effective approach would consider linguistic factors and raise the following questions:

(1) What is the linguistic background of various students? Did they learn Standard English natively, or is Standard English not native to them? (Did they learn a nonstandard dialect of English natively, or is English not their native language?)

(2) What is their family heritage? I draw upon John Ogbu's (1978, 1992) work in this regard; namely, what is their relative immigrant status? Although some issues in Ogbu's work are problematic, I think it is a useful diagnostic in educational contexts.

(3) Did the students' ancestors voluntarily immigrate to the USA, or were they autonomous immigrants? In Ogbu's terms, 'autonomous immigrants' consist of the Jews, Mormons, and the Amish – people who had once been victims of religious discrimination, but who were not so negatively impacted that they remained in poverty in ways that are comparable to involuntary immigrants, including Native Americans and African Americans. One limitation in Ogbu's work, in my opinion, is that he places many Mexican Americans in the involuntary category, despite their voluntary efforts to migrate to the USA. They came seeking better jobs and better opportunities, but they also encountered forms of racial non-White discrimination; I therefore do not think it is appropriate to put them in the involuntary category. They do suffer, but not because they have come here involuntarily.

(4) A student's sexual background is also relevant. Are they male or female? And does their sexual orientation influence their linguistic behavior? Gender has a great deal to do with your opportunities in society.

(5) Are the students under consideration being educated in public or private schools?

Answers to these questions will be important to all educators, but even more so for teachers and educators who work with students who have not had the benefit of learning Standard English as their native dialect.

Title VII regulations define language minority students as those for whom English is not native. But in the Black English trial in 1979, drawing upon statutes contained within Title 20 (i.e. 1703f), Judge Charles Joiner treated nonstandard African American English as if it represented a sufficient language barrier to the academic success of the African American plaintiffs in that case. He did not quibble over whether or not 'Black English' was a dialect or a separate language, but rather that there was a significant language barrier to academic success. And a language barrier need not exist only when someone is speaking a language other than English.

California was actually quite sensitive to this, and in 1981 the California Department of Education implemented the Standard English Proficiency (SEP) Program for students who speak black language. Those programs were extremely well intended and were designed to offer guidelines to educators to help teachers provide Standard English proficiency to African American students. What this did, however, was to create a policy paradox between the federal government (which makes no provision whatsoever for looking at Standard English that is not native) and the SEP Program in California, which – at least in its original incarnation – was focused exclusively on African Americans.

One of the reasons that I did not previously adopt the term Ebonics grows directly from research on the linguistic consequences of American slavery. Although I was aware of Robert Williams' original definition of the term Ebonics, he cast that primordial definition broadly to include slave descendants in the Caribbean and Africa. Readers of this volume may know that Ebonics was first introduced in 1973.

Dr Robert Williams, who invented the term Ebonics, is a psychologist, who first developed the Black Intelligence Test for Cultural Homogeneity (also known as the 'Bitch Test'). The Bitch Test is a standardized test that is biased in favor of African Americans. If you are very familiar with African American culture and our cultural icons, you may do well on the Bitch Test. However, Williams is among the first to admit that his test is biased in favor of African Americans. Ideally, we would prefer testing diagnostics, especially high-stakes testing diagnostics that don't discriminate against anyone. Williams demonstrated that he could create a test that was favorable to African Americans, and he did so prior to coining the term Ebonics.

In his book, titled *Ebonics: The True Language of Black Folks* (1975), Williams described the 'translation process' that he used by substituting words and phrases that were common to the African American experience from standardized tests that were less familiar, from a linguistic and cultural point of view, to most African American students. It was in the context of psychological testing, not original linguistic research, that the term Ebonics was first introduced. Those teachers who have read *Ebonics: The True Language of Black Folks*, will note, as I did, that the majority of contributors to that volume use the term 'Black English' throughout. Why would that be the case? At that time, Ebonics was not a pervasive term; but when you look at Williams' original definition; it includes the linguistic consequences of the slave trade in West Africa, the Caribbean, and the USA. To me, as a linguist, his singular term defies categorization as a single language. Thus, while I have no problem whatsoever with the term Ebonics as it is originally defined, looking at the linguistic consequences of the African slave trade, I do not consider the original Ebonics definition as being synonymous with 'Black English' or 'African American Vernacular English.' If Chomsky (1965) can define universal grammar as applying to all human languages, then I see no reason why Williams cannot create a term that applies to the linguistic consequences of the African slave trade. So I find tremendous value and scholarly utility of Ebonics in reference to the linguistic consequences of the African slave trade, but limited, if not misleading, utility when that definition is restricted only to the linguistic consequences of slavery in the USA.

In later years, however, Dr Ernie Smith (1992) challenged any suggestion that Ebonics was synonymous with Black English or any dialect of English. Indeed, he went so far as to suggest that Ebonics was the antonym of Black English. His subsequent consultation with the Oakland SEP project resulted in some of the controversial wording associated with their Ebonics resolutions, which are likely to be familiar to anyone reading this chapter (see Baugh, 1997, 1998; Rickford, 1997, this volume). Smith's (1992) linguistic assertions helped to create a terminology paradox, because many people have now adopted the term Ebonics without clear specification of their linguistic intentions. Do they seek to equate Ebonics with Black English; do they share Williams' primordial definition regarding the linguistic consequences of the African slave trade; or do they adhere to Smith's (1992) anti-Black English classification? There are competing definitions of Ebonics that are well attested in the literature long before Oakland educators adopted, and eventually abandoned, 'Ebonics' as a linguistic reference for the speech and writing of African American students who attend school within that school district.

Dr John Rickford and I studied with the same professor (William Labov) at the University of Pennsylvania. Labov quite clearly says that to argue that the Black English vernacular is a system completely different from other English systems is 'absurd,' but history has served to shroud the issue. The significant linguistic differences that Judge Joiner attested in his ruling in favor of African American plaintiffs in the Black English trial are not clear-cut, but do they constitute a language other than

English, that is, in contrast to Labov (1972) and in support of Smith (1992)?

Although linguists like me may analyze and debate these matters, it is going to be up to the law and legislators to determine the ultimate legal linguistic classification of American slave descendants. At present, it seems that existing educational regulations do not allow African Americans to be classified as 'language minority students;' that is, despite Judge Joiner's ruling showing that vernacular African American linguistic behavior does stand as a barrier to academic success.

So what do we do with this information? When one ponders the language history of *all* US students and how they are defined by federal regulations, those students for whom English is not native are the only ones who are eligible for Title VII; of those eligible students, only 30% are affected because it is not an entitlement. Title I, for students in poverty, is an entitlement – those funds are authorized automatically. But in order to have access to Title VII funding, students who are not native speakers of English had better be attending a school or a school district that has applied directly to the Federal Government for that funding.

I would like to step back for a moment from the Ebonics controversy as it evolved in Oakland, including their denial of intentions to go after bilingual education funds, and ponder what might have happened had they said, 'Yes, we plan to request bilingual education funding for African American language minority students.' In Baugh (1998) I propose an alternative hypothesis where, within the native English speaking population, one finds two divisions: that is, native Standard English speakers, and individuals for whom Standard English is not native. Under my proposal students who are not native speakers of Standard English would be classified as language minority students. Perhaps some would not be eligible for Title VII funding, but there should be some official recognition of the fact that those who do not speak Standard English require special educational attention. And, of course, students within the traditional classification as language minority students would continue to be eligible for Title VII.

Under this revised classification, what are some other alternative sources of funding one might seek for African American students? In 1994 the Equal Educational Opportunity Act was revised in a manner that would allow educators who receive Title I funding to devote some of those funds to language education through deregulation. Prior to 1994 there were regulatory restrictions on Title I that blocked usage for language education. The previous official presumption was that Title VII would handle educational problems growing from languages other than

English, and Title I would handle educational problems that result from poverty. The revised law recognizes that the problems are not discrete, and that local educators are most likely to be able to identify effective programs that will enhance educational prospects for their students.

Educators have often been constrained by well intended regulations that were supposed to help them at the same time that state and federal legislators were unclear as to how their statutes and mandates were being implemented within schools. Should educators alter educational standards for the poor, or for those who do not speak English, or should educational programs be adapted to help less fortunate students compete more effectively with affluent students who have learned Standard English natively? In short, I endorse the latter, believing that educational flexibility and adaptability are vital to the educational welfare of most low income and minority students, although many educational regulations – and limited resources – make this task most daunting.

As a former director of Stanford's teacher education program I have tried to help future teachers recognize that they must do their very best to be effective with students from all walks of life, not merely those with whom they feel most comfortable. This too can be a daunting task for those educators who can not free themselves from the pervasive stereotypes that plague less fortunate students, but the difficulty of this task should not dissuade us from its importance, and I am pleased – indeed honored – to present these observations with readers and colleagues who share a vision of equitable education, refuting that 'one size fits all,' but that effective education may vary considerably depending upon the personal background, history, and preferred learning styles of less fortunate students.

The education of low income and minority students in inner city and rural schools is among the most difficult of all teaching assignments. And those of us who have been involved with teacher education share some of the responsibility, if not a portion of the blame, for not adequately pointing out specific instances of similarities and difference that teachers who teach in classrooms with minimal linguistic diversity, and teachers who teach in classrooms where students' linguistic backgrounds vary, will encounter. The latter task tends to be far more complicated, and yet these are often the very classrooms that are constrained by limited resources or by inexperienced teachers who are simply overwhelmed by a plethora of other problems that severely restrict their capacity to teach.

Rather than repeat suggestions that appear elsewhere in this volume, I would encourage readers to share this book with other educators, parents, and legislators of good will who seek to break the perpetual cycles of educational failure that have harmed previous generations of poor students, in favor of some of the excellent ideas that appear throughout this book and elsewhere (see Cleary & Linn, 1993; Darling-Hammond, 1997; Hollins *et al.*, 1994).

The ultimate goal remains the same: we seek to provide educational opportunities that will allow all children the chance to achieve to the best of their ability, and in so doing allow them to become good citizens who have the capacity to help themselves, their families, and the welfare of others.

References

Baugh, J. (1997) What's in a name? That by which we call the linguistic consequences of the African slave trade. *The Quarterly of the National Writing Project* 19 (9).

Baugh, J. (1998) Linguistics, education, and the law: Educational reform for African American language minority students. In S.S. Mufwene, J. Rickford, G. Baile and J. Baugh (eds) *African American English: History, Structure, and Usage*. London: Routledge.

Chomsky, N. (1965) *Aspects of a Theory of Syntax*. Cambridge, MA: MIT Press.

Cleary, L.M. and Linn, M.D. (eds) (1993) *Linguistics for Teachers*. New York: McGraw Hill.

Darling-Hammond, L. (1997) *A Right to Learn*. San Francisco: Jossey-Bass.

Hollins, E., King, J. and Haymen, W. (eds) (1994) *Teaching Diverse Populations: Formulating a Knowledge Base*. Albany: State University of New York Press.

Labov, W. (1972) *Language in the Inner-city: Studies in the Black English Vernacular*. Philadelphia: University of Pennsylvania Press.

Ogbu, J. (1978) *Minority Education and Caste*. New York: Academic Press.

Ogbu, J. (1992) Understanding cultural diversity and learning. *Educational Researcher* November 5–14.

Rickford, J. (1997) Suite for ebony and phonics. *Discover Magazine*.

Smith, E. (1992) African American language behavior: A world of difference. In E.H. Dryer (ed.) *Claremont Reading Conference* (pp. 39–53). Pomona: Claremont College.

Williams, R. (1975) *Ebonics. The True Language of Black Folks*. St. Louis: Robert Williams and Associates.

Black Language and the Education of Black Children: One Mo Once[1]

GENEVA SMITHERMAN

> We have had pronouncements on Black speech from the NAACP...
> from highly publicized scholars... from executives of national
> corporations... from housewives and community folk. I mean, really,
> it seem like everybody and they momma done had something to say
> on the subject!

The above words were NOT written in the wake of the 1996 Oakland,
California School Board's resolution on Ebonics. Rather this quotation
comes from my first major publication on black speech, *Talkin and
Testifyin: The Language of Black America*, which was published back in
1977. As in the past, today's negative pronouncements on Ebonics reveal
a serious lack of knowledge about the scientific approach to language
analysis as well as galling ignorance about what Ebonics is (more than
'slang') and who speaks it (at some point in their lives, 90% of African
Americans). Most critically, these pronouncements actually reveal an
appalling rejection of the language of everyday Black people. See, when
you lambast the home language that kids bring to school, you ain just
dissin dem, you talkin bout they mommas! Check out the concept of
'*Mother* Tongue.'

Although the late Roy Wilkins (of the NAACP) once declared that
'Black English is black nonsense' (1971), that was before the accumula-
tion and widespread dissemination of a massive body of research on
Black Language which attests incontrovertibly to its existence, dynamism
and systematicity (see, e.g. Asante, 1972, 1990; Baugh, 1983, 2000; Dalby,
1969, 1970, 1972; Dillard, 1972, 1977; Fasold & Shuy, 1970; Kochman,
1972, 1981; Labov, 1970, 1972; Major, 1970, 1994; Rickford, 1991, 2000;
Smitherman, 1977, 1981a, 2000; Spears, 1982; Taylor, 1991; Williams, 1975;
Wolfram, 1970).

In the 1980s, there emerged a critical mass of Sistas writing in the Black Language Thang and winning mainstream literary prizes for these works (e.g. Alice Walker's Pulitzer Prize for *The Color Purple* written almost entirely in Black English). In 1979, Black Language was legally recognized in Judge Charles C. Joiner's federal ruling in *King* (the so-called 'Ann Arbor Black English' case; see e.g. Smitherman, 1981b). Since at least the 1960s, there has been continuing big-time crossover of Black Language into the nation's public discourse as well as intellectual analysis of this crossover. I mean there is a tradition of research on this subject that contemporary know-nothings could have gone to the library and read – like they bees tellin black youth to do!

At this late stage in history, how is it that people are still missing the beat on Black Language? Yeah, uhm sayin 'language,' cause I think it is a language. Anyway, as the linguist Weinreich said over half a century ago, the only difference between a language and a dialect is who's got the army and the navy! This article will seek to drop some knowledge on the subject of Black Language – one mo once.

Where 'Ebonics' Come From?

In the month after the Oakland School Board's resolution, the term 'Ebonics' turned 24 years old. It was coined by a group of Black scholars, principal among them clinical psychologist, Dr Robert L. Williams, at a conference on language and the Black child, convened in St. Louis, Missouri in January, 1973. In the preface to the book of conference proceedings that Dr Williams edited, which was published in 1975 by the independent Institute of Black Studies in St. Louis, he writes:

> A significant incident occurred at the conference. The black conferees were so critical of the work on the subject done by white researchers, many of whom also happened to be present, that they decided to caucus among themselves and define black language from a black perspective. It was in this caucus that the term Ebonics was created.

In the book's introduction, Williams goes on to amplify this terminology, defining Ebonics as:

> ...the linguistic and paralinguistic features which on a concentric continuum represents the communicative competence of the West African, Caribbean, and United States slave descendants of African origin. It includes the various idioms, patois, argots, ideolects, and social dialects of black people, especially those who have been forced to adapt to colonial circumstances. 'Ebonics' derives its form from

ebony (black) and phonics (sound, the study of sound) and refers to the study of the language of black people in all its cultural uniqueness.

Somehow or other (*somehow*?) the concept of a linguistic continuum and the terminology to express that concept, as created by these black scholars, never caught on in the academic world. After only a few years, Williams's book went out of print, and the linguistic–cultural practices of US slave descendants continued to be referred to as 'Black English' or 'Black Vernacular English,' updated in the 1990s to 'African American (Vernacular) English.' Nonetheless it is fortunate that Williams had the wisdom and vision to write it all down, to publish the spirit and essence of those conference proceedings and preserve the historical record in the Black voice.

It is clear that Williams and the other Black scholars convened there in St. Louis in 1973 viewed Ebonics as a superordinate term, covering all the African–European language mixtures developed in the various African–European language contact situations throughout the world. That is, they were using the term to refer to, say, Haitian Creole, a West African–French language mixture, as well as to the Dutch Creole spoken in Suriname, as well as to Jamaican Creole, West African Pidgin English, etc., etc. – and, of course, to the West African–English mixture spoken in the USA. This superordinate concept symbolizes the linguistic unity of the Black World and locates Black American English/US Ebonics (USEB) within an African linguistic–cultural context. Most importantly for our purposes here, the Ebonics conceptual framework lays the foundation for a multilingual instructional policy that begins with the Mother Tongue, which is conventional pedagogy in language teaching and would not have caused a blip on the social radar screen had not race been involved.

When the Oakland School Board tapped into the Ebonics framework, they were seeking an alternative pedagogical paradigm to redress the noneducation of Black youth in their school district. We should applaud their refusal to continue doing more of the same that has not worked in the past. Speaking of which, how come ain none of dese Black so-call 'leaders' raise no sand bout the lack of literacy among Black youth? Seem to me dat's where they ought to be puttin they energy instead of doggin' those Oakland school folk!

Definition Of Ebonics – What It Be Like?

Ebonics is not 'broken English,' nor is it 'sloppy speech' – terms which linguists do not apply to any language, or language variety, because all languages are systematic, rule-governed, and predictable. Although 'slang' constitutes a small part of the Ebonics spoken in this country, USEB is more than 'slang,' which refers to forms of speech that are highly transitory and limited to specific subgroups, e.g. today's Hip Hoppers. However, in USEB, words and idioms which are 'slang' today become part of the general lexicon of the Black speech community tomorrow. Anybody from eight to eighty knows that in Black Talk, there are two 'kitchens,' only one of which has to do with cooking. Despite the recent near-hysteria about Black Language, street people, gangstas, or baggy-pants-wearing teens are only *some* of the speakers of USEB. All kinds of other folk speak US Ebonics, like blue and white-collar working adults, the congregations of the churches, owners of barbershops, beauty shops, and other small businesses, our elders, young children, etc.

USEB is a communication system with its own morphology, syntax, phonology, and rhetorical and semantic strategies. Consider the statement, 'The Brotha be lookin good; that's what got the Sista nose open!' 'Brotha' is USEB for an African American man, 'lookin good' refers to his style, his attractive appearance (not necessarily the same thing as physical beauty in USEB), 'Sista' is USEB for an African American woman, and her passionate love for the Brotha is conveyed by the phrase 'nose open' (in USEB, the kind of passionate love that makes you vulnerable to exploitation). The use of 'be' means that the quality of 'lookin good' is not limited to the present moment, but reflects the Brotha's past, present, and future essence. As in the case of Efik and other Niger-Congo languages, USEB has an aspectual verb system, conveyed by the use of the English verb 'be' to denote iterativity (that is, a recurring or habitual state-of-affairs). Note further that folk like Black writers and today's Rap artists employ the spellings 'Brotha' and 'Sista.' They ain' just tryin to be cute. These orthographic representations are used to convey the systematic phonological pattern of post-vocalic *r* deletion (i.e. 'r-lessness' after vowels). Also in many West African language communities, kinship terms are used when referring to African people, whether biologically related or not.

But this is not all there is to Ebonics. It is also a certain, Africanized style of using European languages, a system of communicative practices. Take, for instance, *Signification*, or more commonly, *signifyin*. In using this rhetorical and semantic strategy, which can be spoken with or without the phonological and morphosyntactical patterns of Ebonics, the speaker deploys exaggeration, irony, and indirection. Signification is a way of saying something on two different levels at once. It is often used to send a message of social critique, a bit of social commentary on the action or statements of someone who is in need of a wake-up call. When signifyin is done with verbal dexterity, it avoids the creation of social distance between speaker and audience because the rich humor makes you laugh to keep from crying. Like Malcolm X who once began a speech with these words: 'Mr. Moderator, Brother Lomax, Brothers and Sisters, friends and enemies.' Now, you do not usually begin a speech by addressing your enemies. Thus, Malcolm's signifyin statement signaled to his audience that he knew inimical forces were out there. Or like one of the deacons at this traditional black church, where the preacher would never deal with the problems and issues folk were facing on a daily basis. Rather, he was always preachin bout the pearly gates and how great thangs was gon be at dat home up in the sky. So one day this deacon said to the preacher, 'Reb, I got a home in Heaven, but I ain't homesick.'

Although Reverend Jesse Jackson and Maya Angelou came out in the national news and 'dissed' the Oakland School Board's resolution, both are well versed in USEB, and they are verbal geniuses when it comes to manipulating Black Language to score points. (To his credit, Jackson later reversed himself.) In *Talkin and Testifyin*, I wrote about and quoted from them as linguistic role models that our youth could aspire to emulate. Like Jesse who is down wit the Tonal Semantics and Signification of USEB: 'Pimp, punk, prostitute, preacher, Ph.D. – all the P's, you still in slavery!' He also uses copula absence here – 'you still in slavery' – which has not been found in any of the dialects of British English that came over on the Mayflower, but which is used widely in the languages of West Africa.

'Playin the Dozens' is a type of signifyin in which speakers play a game of ritualized verbal insult of each other's mommas (or other relatives, but usually mothers). Sometimes called 'snappin' by today's Hip Hoppers, the Dozens is like 'Yo momma so dumb she thought a quarterback was a refund!' Well, Sista Maya is so bad she don't play the Dozens, she play the Thirteens! She uses this Black Language pattern to critique the actions of blacks and whites. Here how she do it:

(The Thirteens Black):
Your Momma took to shouting
Your Poppa's gone to war,
Your sister's in the streets
Your brother's in the bar,
The thirteens. Right On...
And you, you make me sorry
You out here by yourself,

I'd call you something dirty,
But there just ain't nothing left,
cept
The thirteens. Right On...
(The Thirteens White):
Your daughter wears a jock strap,
Your son he wears a bra
Your brother jonesed your cousin
in the back seat of the car.
The thirteens. Right On...
Your money thinks you're something
But if I'd learned to curse,
I'd tell you what your name is
But there just ain't nothing worse
than The Thirteens. Right On...
(Excerpts taken from Angelou's collection, *Just Give Me a Cool Drink of Water 'Fore I Diiie*, 1971)

USEB reflects the transformation of ancient elements of African languages, intertwined with American-style English, into a new language forged in the crucible of enslavement, Southern-style apartheid, racism, and the struggle to survive and thrive in the face of domination. From its beginning as a *pidgin* (a language mixture) during the slave trade, this system of communication served both as a transactional language between captors and captives, neither of whom could speak the other's language, and as a *lingua franca* among enslaved Africans of diverse ethnic backgrounds. Although 'Ole Massa' would mix up Africans from different linguistic backgrounds on his plantation in order to foil communication and thwart escape, the Africans appropriated the foreign tongue and reconstructed it as a counter language by superimposing their own linguistic practices upon the white man's speech. When an enslaved African said 'Everybody talkin bout Heaben ain goin dere,' it was a double-voiced form of speech which signified on slaveholders who professed Christianity but practiced slavery. Thus, USEB has provided a code for Africans in America to talk about black business, publicly or privately, and in the enslavement period, even to talk about 'Massa' himself right in front of his face.

Who Done Study Ebonics? – The Research Tradition

Research on US-style Ebonics can be traced back at least as far as 1884 when James A. Harrison published a 47-page description of 'Negro

English' in the journal *Anglia*. Harrison's description of the 'Negro English' of the 19th century, which he described as an 'outline of Negro language-usage,' though racist in its perceptive, clearly acknowledges that this 'Negro language-usage' is African-derived. It is just that, as far as Harrison was concerned, the Africanness in the language was pathological. Thus Harrison argued that 'Negro English' lacked linguistic resources, for instance, the interdental fricative sound *th*. Scientifically speaking, however, no language 'lacks' linguistic resources. I mean, just because English doesn't have all the clicks that former South African President Nelson Mandela has in his native Xhosa, is English deficient?

Dr Lorenzo Dow Turner, the first Black American linguist, decades after Harrison, based upon his knowledge of the languages of West Africa, was to explain that such linguistic phenomena as the interdental fricative *th* sound did not exist in West African languages. It took Dr Turner nearly 20 years to complete and publish his work on the Gullah Language, that form of Ebonics spoken on the Sea Islands and in parts of South Carolina and Georgia. Those two decades were spent mastering several African languages and immersing himself in the Gullah speech community, both tasks which Turner felt to be a *sine qua non* for doing the research he had committed himself to. Further, the time span was drawn out because Turner made his own phonograph records to record the language data he collected. (This Brotha was on a mission!)

Africanisms in the Gullah Dialect is the title of Turner's 1949 book on Gullah style Ebonics. He found at least 4000 words of direct African origin, and he demonstrated the African linguistic survivals in American English, for example, words such as *tote*, *gorilla*, *gumbo*, *jazz*, and *cola* (as in 'coca-cola'). He also found syntactical and phonological patterns in Gullah which were attributable to African language influence, such as using the same form of a noun for singular or plural, as in *one dog*, *five dog*, (a pattern found in Ibo, for example), and substituting a *d* or *t* for the English *th*, depending on whether the *th* is voiced or voiceless. Turner wrote:

> Whenever the native West African today first encounters the English *th* sounds, whether in the United States, the Caribbean, West Africa, or elsewhere, he at first substitutes for them [d] and [t] with which he is thoroughly familiar and which he considers closer to the English *th* than any of the sounds of his language. This is true whether he is literate or illiterate. All of my African informants who have recently learned to speak English use these substitutes, and it is reasonable to suppose that their ancestors who came to South Carolina and

Georgia direct from Africa as slaves reacted similarly to the English *th* sounds when encountering them for the first time.

In the 1960s, research on Ebonics exploded, initiated in 1965 by late Dr Beryl Bailey, who hailed from Jamaica and began her university career at Hunter College in New York City. Now, Bailey does not get the credit she deserves, but it was this first Black woman linguist who reintroduced the concept of a linguistic continuum from Africa to the Caribbean and North America in the Diaspora (Bailey, 1965). I say 'reintroduced' because Turner's book went out of print amidst national attacks on the concept of African survivals in Black American language and culture; attacks led, unfortunately, by Black scholars like sociologist Dr E. Franklin Frazier.

Dr Bailey immediately began to apply her theoretical postulates about Jamaican speech and US Ebonics to the education of Blacks both on the public school and college levels. She worked with prefreshmen at Tougaloo college in Mississippi in 1965 and developed a program for teaching academic discourse to speakers of USEB. It was a program that she based 'directly on a knowledge of the... dialect [which was] likely to be much more efficient and economical than programs that regard a standard spoken as the norm' (Bailey, 1968). She sought to explode myths and misconceptions that teachers had about Black children's abilities and called for revisions of the language arts curriculum and Black language-specific instructional strategies for Black children (Bailey, 1969).

Long before literary theorists recovered the vernacular tradition in African American literature, Bailey made a case for the linguistic reliability of the Black writer's ear and extrapolated language data from literature. It was (and is) an unconventional method in the field of linguistics, but one that can provide authentic representations of Black speech data that might otherwise be inaccessible to the researcher (cause Brothas and Sistas don't be wontin to talk into no tape recorders). Making the case for intellectual boldness and keeping it real, way back in 1965, Bailey put it this way:

> I was compelled to modify the orthodox procedures and even, at times, to adopt some completely unorthodox ones... This may sound like hocus-pocus, but... a hocus-pocus procedure which yields the linguistic facts is surely preferable to a scientifically rigorous one which murders those facts.

Dr Beryl Bailey's untimely death would leave US Ebonics research to be mined by European-American male linguists. The work of these white scholars successfully challenged prevailing notions and myths about Black linguistic inferiority (see, especially, William Labov's ground-breaking *The Study of Nonstandard English*, 1970).

British linguist David Dalby set the European-American world on fire when he presented his research findings, written up in academic publications as well as in the *New York Times*, about what he referred to as the 'African element in American English' (1969, 1970, 1972). Dalby argued that even *okay* has its roots in West African languages (the use of *kay*, especially after words meaning 'yes,' as in Wolof, *waw kay*, Mandingo, *o-k$_\epsilon$* meaning 'yes indeed'). Other examples cited by Dalby include: *bug*, as in the older USEB idiom, 'That *bugs* me,' and in today's Hip Hop phrase, *buggin out*, and the ever-popular *bad*, through semantic inversion from Mandingo, *a ka nyi ko-jugu*, referring to something that is good badly, or it's so good that it's bad. It is as James Baldwin said back in 1979, in his *New York Times* essay, 'If Black English Isn't a Language, Then Tell Me What Is?' American English would be shonuf wack without contributions from USEB. Doan know why sometime we Black folk be actin like we ain got sense enough to know what we got!

To be sure, the research done by many of the white linguists had some limitations, as those Black scholars at that 1973 conference also noted. For one thing, some of this work presented only the sensational, street culture aspects of Black Language. For another, the work was heavily maleocentric, completely ignoring the voices of Black women. Sometime, though, I guess you got to take the bitter wit the sweet. Cause the research of these white linguists (given the high credibility automatically associated with their gender and race) contributed significantly to the eradication of stereotypes and the misconception that Ebonics speakers suffered from linguistic-cognitive deficiencies.

From 1977 to 1979, working as chief advocate and expert witness for a group of single parent Black mothers in Ann Arbor, Michigan, I was able to help them win a Federal court case to salvage the education of their children. The school district was ordered to stop using the children's language as the basis to put them into learning disability classes and as the basis to set up low expectations for what these children could learn. In Judge Charles C. Joiner's Memorandum and Opinion, he acknowledged the legitimacy of Black English and ordered the school district to train its teachers. On July 12, 1979, Judge Joiner wrote:

> It is clear that black children who succeed, and many do, learn to be bilingual. They retain fluency in 'black English' to maintain status in the community and they become fluent in standard English to

succeed in the general society... no matter how well intentioned the teachers are, they are not likely to be successful in overcoming the language barrier caused by their failure to take into account the home language system, unless they are helped... to recognize the existence of the language system used by the children in their home community and to use that knowledge as a way of helping the children to learn to read standard English.

Owing to the undue negative influence of Black 'leaders,' there have been few studies applying the Ebonics conceptual framework to the acquisition of literacy in the Language of Wider Communication ('Standard English'). A pilot research project was conducted by Simpkins and Simpkins (1974) for the reading series they developed along with late linguist Dr Grace Holt, which they entitled *Bridge*. Capitalizing on the linguistic competence of Black youth, this work took students from 'Black Vernacular' to 'Standard English' readers. The Simpkins team supervised 14 teachers and 27 classes, involving 540 students, in experimental and control groups, over a four-month period, in five areas: Chicago, Illinois; Phoenix, Arizona; Washington DC; Memphis, Tennessee; and Macon County, Alabama. Using the standardized Iowa Test of Basic Skills in Reading Comprehension to assess gains in reading, the researchers found that the experimental/Bridge groups made a gain of 6.2 months in their reading over the four-month period, whereas the non-Bridge groups, who were taught via the traditional method, with no focus on their home language, only gained 1.6 months in the four months of instruction. This latter result is what we see in urban Black districts today, and what Oakland is struggling against, namely the longer Black kids stay in school, the further behind they get. Despite these spectacular results, *Bridge* was never implemented because like I said, boojy Black 'leaders' killed the idea.

So What We Gon Do?

Let us consult the Elders. In 1967, psychiatrist Dr Frantz Fanon wrote: 'Every dialect, every language, is a way of thinking. To speak means to assume a culture.' Thus, according to Fanon, those blacks who get educated need to express theyself in the community language to make it plain that nothing done change. In his classic 1933 study, *The Miseducation of the Negro*, Dr Carter G. Woodson said that Black children need to study our language as an African tongue that had been 'broken down' by the conditions of enslavement. Woodson also argued that the educational system did not meet the needs of Black or white students, an inadequacy that lingers still today. Over half a century ago, Dr W.E.B. Du Bois called for African-centered education in the Mother Tongue: 'A French university uses the French language and assumes a knowledge of French history. In the same way, a Negro university in the United States of America begins with Negroes. It uses that variety of the English idiom which they understand.'

Building on the wisdom of the Elders, the Ebonics research tradition, and the global needs of the 21st century, I propose that we work for a national multilingual policy and a progressive educational program for all children educated in the USA. African Americans, because of our long and continuous history of struggle around language and power issues, should take the leadership in this struggle.

The multilingual policy I am advocating must include ALL of the following elements – any one of these, implemented alone, is insufficient to prepare the next generation of youth: (1) the Language of Wider Communication, English, because it is on its way to becoming the global *lingua franca*; (2) a foreign language, either an African language spoken widely on the Continent, where the everyday people do not speak English (or French), or Spanish because of the large number of Spanish speakers not only in this country but also in the Caribbean and other parts of this hemisphere; and (3) preservation and enhancement of competence in the Mother Tongue – whatever language it may be – because it is the base of individual and group identity. (This aspect of the policy would provide a prime opportunity for European Americans to develop greater fluency in the languages that are part of their heritage.)

This national multilingual policy should be part of the preparation of the next generation for world citizenship. But it must be framed within a progressive educational philosophy that asks and answers the question: 'Education for what?' Education cannot be just for individual gittin ovah, that is, just to enter the mainstream and continue on with business as usual. Rather I am talking about multilingualism within an educational framework for social change. I am talkin about promoting a vision of community and social responsibility in the next generation, who, as Fanon said, 'must, out of relative obscurity, discover its mission, fulfill it, or betray it.'

Notes

1. This article first appeared in *The Black Scholar* 27 (1). Reprinted with permission.

References

Asante, M.K. [formerly known as Smith, Arthur] (ed.) (1972) *Language, Communication and Rhetoric in Black America*. New York: Harper & Row.

Asante, M.K. (1990) African elements in African-American English. In J. Holloway (ed.) *Africanisms in American Culture*. Bloomington, IN: Indiana University Press.

Bailey, B.L. (1965) Toward a new perspective in Negro English dialectology. *American Speech* 40 (3), 170–177.

Bailey, B.L. (1968) Some aspects of the impact of linguistics on language teaching in disadvantaged communities. In A.L. Davis (ed.) *On the Dialects of Children* (pp. 15–24). Champaign: The National Council of Teachers of English.

Bailey, B.L. (1969) Language and communicative styles of Afro-American children in the United States. *The Florida FL Reporter* Spring/Summer, 46, 153

Baugh, J. (1983) *Black Street Speech: It's History, Structure, and Survival*. Austin, TX: University of Texas Press.

Dalby, D. (1969) *Black Through White: Patterns of Communication in Africa and the New World*. Bloomington: Indiana University Press.

Dalby, D. (1970) Jazz, fitter and jam. *The New York Times* November 10.

Dalby, D. (1972) The African element in American English. In T. Kochman (ed.) *Rappin' and Stylin' Out: Communication in Urban Black America*. Chicago: University of Illinois Press.

Dillard, J.L. (1972) *Black English*. New York: Random House.

Dillard, J.L. (1977) *Lexicon of Black English*. New York: The Seabury Press.

Du Bois, W.E.B. (1933) The field and function of the Negro college. In A. Aptheker (ed.) *The Education of Black People: Ten Critiques – 1906–1960*. Amherst, MA: The University of Massachusetts Press.

Fanon, E. (1967) *The Negro and Language – Black Skin, White Masks*. New York: Grove Press Inc.

Fasold, R.W. and Shuy, R.W. (eds) (1970) *Teaching Standard English in the Inner City*. Washington, DC: Center for Applied Linguistics.

Harrison, J.A. (1984) Negro English. *Anglia* 7, 232–279.

Kochman, T. (ed.) (1972) *Rapping' and Stylin' Out. Communication in Urban Black America*. Urbana, IL: University of Illinois Press.

Kochman, T. (1981) *Black and White – Styles in Conflict*. Chicago, IL: The University of Chicago Press.

Labov, W. (1970) *The Study of Nonstandard English*. Champaign, IL: National Council of Teachers of English.

Labov, W. (1972) *Language in the Inner City. Studies in the Black English Vernacular*. Philadelphia: The University of Pennsylvania Press, Inc.

Major, C. (1970) *Dictionary of Afro-American Slang*. New York: International Publishers.

Major, C. (1994) (ed.) *Juba to Jove – A Dictionary of African-American Slang*. New York: Penguin Books USA Inc.

Rickford, J.R., Ball, A.F., Blake, R., Jackson, R. and Martin, N. (1991) Rappin' on the copula coffin: Theoretical and methodological issues in the analysis of copula variation in African-American Vernacular English. *Language Variation and Change* 3 (1), 103–132.

Simpkins, G. and Simpkins, C. (1974) Cross-cultural approach to curriculum development. In G. Smitherman (ed.) (1981) *Black English and the Education of Black Children and Youth* (pp. 212–240). Detroit: Wayne State University Center for Black Studies.

Smitherman, G. (1977 & 1986) *Talkin and Testifyin.* Detroit, MI: Wayne State University Press.

Smitherman, G. (1981a) *Black English and the Education of Black Children and Youth.* Detroit, MI: Wayne State University Center for Black Studies.

Smitherman, G. (1981b) 'What Go Round Come Round': King in Perspective. *Harvard Educational Review* 51 (1), 40–56.

Smitherman, G. (1994) *Black Talk.* Boston: Houghton Mifflen.

Spears, A.K. (1982) The Black English semi-auxiliary come. *Language* 58 (4), 850–872.

Taylor, H.U. (1991) *Standard English, Black English, and Bidialectalism – A Controversy.* New York: Peter Lang Publishing, Inc.

Turner, L.D. (1949) *Africansms in the Gullah Dialect.* Chicago: University of Chicago Press.

US District Judge Charles C. Joiner (1979) Memorandum Opinion and Order, Civil Action No. 7-71861, 473 F. Supp. 1371, July 12.

Wilkins, R. (1971) Black Nonsense. *Crisis* 78.

Williams, R.L. (ed.) (1975) *Ebonics: The True Language of Black Folks.* St. Louis: Institute of Black Studies.

Wolfram, W.A. (1970) *A Sociolinguistic Description of Detroit Negro Speech.* Washington, DC: Center for Applied Linguistics.

Woodson, C. (1933) *Miseducation of the Negro.* Washington, DC: Associated Publishers.

Ebonics and Education in the Context of Culture: Meeting the Language and Cultural Needs of English Learning African American Students

SUBIRA KIFANO and ERNIE A. SMITH

Introduction

The question of whether there are cultural and linguistic differences in and between the various cultural/ethnic groups in America has been more or less reconciled on the part of educational policymakers and educators. Generally, there is agreement that there are differences. However, still extensively debated are the bases for these differences, a delineation of those differences, and the extent to which these differences affect the academic achievement of students in public schools where Standard American English (SAE) is the language of instruction.

When a critical review is made of the literature on African American speech, one finds that although there is considerable debate about what one should call the speech of African American people (i.e. African American Speech, Black English Vernacular, Ebonics, African American English or African American Language), there is no dispute as to whether the language spoken by African American people and SAE are different. Professionals who work with African American children in public and private schools have advanced numerous approaches to reconcile the differences in order to positively affect the academic achievement of these students. While some approaches have produced small gains in the achievement of African American students, the question remains, how can significant, systemic change be made? We contend the reasons there are such small changes lie in the limited application of culturally grounded theories about African American speech.

A review of the literature reveals that many of these theories were derived to explain the origins of African American Ebonics (AAE) in the hope that knowledge of the origin would help explain the differences in the language of African American students and SAE, the language of instruction in public and private schools. Even though many educators gave credence to a variety of paradigms contained in several theories, their approaches seldom fully implemented the prescriptions advanced in such theories. For our purposes here, we will discuss the Africologist/ Ethnolinguistic theory (Smith, 1994) of the origins and historical development of African American Language, which has offered prescriptions currently being implemented in the Los Angeles Unified School District's Academic English Mastery Program (AEMP) and the Mary McLeod Bethune Institute (MMBI). This paper will first delineate the Africologist/Ethnolinguistic theory in contrast with the Transformationalist and Dialectologist theories and then present an overview of its application in the AEMP and the MMBI.

Origins of African American Ebonics – The Africologist/ Ethnolinguistic Theory

Commonly called 'Africologists,' the proponents of the Africologist/ Ethnolinguistic theory on the origin and historical development of African American speech are scholars and researchers whose focus is primarily on the study of African cultures and languages. The term 'Africologist' is used to distinguish the African (continental African and African American, i.e. Black) scholars who posit an African-centered view of the descendants of enslaved Africans' language, from scholars known as 'Africanists' that study African peoples and languages. There are some Africanists who share the Africologist view. Scholars who specialize in language and culture are also called Ethnolinguists.

The view of the Africologists is that while the precolonial contacts between Africans and Europeans are important in the backward tracing of the linguistic history of ancient African and African American people, what is at issue is not to which ancient aboriginal African language family African American speech originally belonged. The issue is, relative to the much more recent historical contacts and linguistic convergence that occurred between the colonial European and Niger-Congo African people, to which language family is contemporary African American speech more akin? That is, is Afro-American speech more akin to the Indo-European or the African language family?

The branch of linguistics that studies 'short term shifts and long-term changes in the sound system, grammar and vocabulary of one or more languages is called historical linguistics' (Hartmann & Stork, 1976). Also known as comparative linguistics and diachronic linguistics, the *Dictionary of Language and Linguistics* (Hartmann & Stork, 1976) states that comparative linguistics is:

> ... an approach to language studies in which states of phonological, grammatical and lexical correspondences between related languages between different periods in the historical development of one language are listed and classified (p. 43)... historical phonology is concerned with sound change, historical grammar with changes in morphology and syntax; and historical semantics with change in meanings of lexical items. Historical linguistics is traditionally linked with comparative philology which studies structural affinities between languages with the aim of finding their common ancestor language. (p. 104)

The Africologists contend that in contemporary historical and comparative linguistics, there are three methods of classification that have been variously and cogently used, the 'genetic,' the 'areal,' and the 'typological.' Although all three of these methods are quite legitimate and equally valid, within the limits for which they are qualified and used, it is only the 'genetic' method that classifies languages based on 'common origins' and then predicates linguistic kinship on empirical evidence of retained and transmitted linguistic forms. As Greenberg (1967: 66) states:

> Classification based on common origin is, as has been seen, fundamental for historical and comparative linguistics. Its importance is so obvious that when language classification is referred to without further qualification, it is genetic comparison that is normally meant. Yet there are other equally legitimate methods of language classification useful for other purposes. Confusion results only when a classification reached by one method is erroneously treated as an exemplification of one of the other methods, thus leading to invalid inferences... There are three methods of language classification which are of major significance: the genetic, the typological, and the areal. Of these, the genetic is the only one which is at once non-arbitrary, exhaustive, and unique... This is because genetic classification reflects historical events which must have occurred or not occurred.

Based on their comparative linguistic studies and findings, the Africologists contend that African American speech is the linguistic continuation of Africa in an African American context. That is, African American speech is both 'typologically' and 'genetically' African. This prompts the questions, what precisely is meant by the term 'typologically' and upon what specific criteria or transmitted linguistic features is 'genetic kinship' evidenced? According to Joseph Greenberg (1967: 66):

> Typological classifications are based on criteria of sound without meaning, meaning without sound, or both... Typological classifications are arbitrary because any criteria or combination of criteria may be used with consistent results, provided only that they have clear meaning when applied to diverse languages... There is in most cases a tendency for genetically related languages to belong to the same type, but there will be exceptions.

As Greenberg has noted, typological classifications are exhaustive and they are unique. But, as he also states, they are arbitrary. Depending on the level of structure being considered, some languages can be the same type phonologically, a different type morphologically and yet another type syntactically. Thus, the classification of languages by type is actually more a matter of degree rather than an absolute category. As a method for the description of particular features and properties of languages, the typological method is elucidating. However, a vital weakness of typological classifications is that languages of different origins and unrelated, based on one criteria, can be confused as being akin based on another.

Areal classifications designate a geographical 'area' where a particular language or group of languages exists. 'They are neither exhaustive nor unique' (Greenberg, 1967: 68). Like typological classifications, areal classifications are arbitrary. Firstly in that, as a result of historical migrations, a number of languages can share the same region. As 'languages in contact practically always affect one another in some way' (Greenberg, 1967: 67), a decision as to whether they are related or unrelated is a matter of criteria. Secondly, even if political restrictions are of no consequence, the very selection of the geographical boundaries for conducting a language study in terms of where the study will begin and where the study will end is a judgment call (i.e. arbitrary).

'Genetic' classification, on the other hand, is nonarbitrary. That is, 'there is no choice of criteria leading to different and equally legitimate results' (Greenberg, 1967: 66). As Greenberg (1967: 67) states:

Genetic classification... is based on criteria of sound-meaning resemblances of linguistic forms. Related languages are likely to be in the same geographical region but usually are not in continuous distribution. In principle, geography is irrelevant, although it is a normal result that related languages are in the same general area... Were people to be discovered on the moon speaking a language with the vocabulary and grammar of English, a conclusion of genetic relationship would perforce be drawn, regardless of geographical circumstances.

The above postulation made by Greenberg that, 'genetic classification... is based on criteria of sound-meaning resemblances of linguistic forms,' is of crucial significance. For, one can infer from the statement that genetic kinship is based on criteria of shared vocabulary and shared meanings. This interpretation would mean that when people use the same words and mean the same thing, their language is genetically the same.

However, contend the Africologists, the notion that it is shared vocabulary and a shared meaning that makes language genetically related would be grossly inaccurate. For, it is not difficult to find instances every day where persons who are from totally different linguistic backgrounds can communicate with each other by using the same words to convey the same meanings. The ability to communicate via shared vocabulary and a shared meaning does not in any way make the native language of these people genetically related. The only thing the ability to communicate via shared vocabulary and a shared meaning establishes is that there is 'mutual intelligibility' between two speakers. That is, while it may be the case that when two people use the same words and mean the same thing that they are speaking the same language, being able to speak the same language is one thing. Being speakers of native languages that are genetically related is quite another. The Africologists contend that, when people whose native languages are totally different are capable of engaging in a mutually intelligible conversation, they are able to communicate because an 'interactive bilingualism' exists. Put simply, they are both or at least one of them is bilingual. This would be precisely what occurs when a native Korean-speaking storekeeper communicates with a native Spanish-speaking Latino customer in English. Likewise when African Americans who speak Ebonics communicate with a Korean storekeeper or Spanish-speaking restaurant owner in English, this does not make the native language (Ebonics) of African Americans genetically related to Korean,

Spanish or English. More precisely, they are for the purposes of communication using English as a lingua franca.

The Africologists contend that in the field of comparative linguistics in order to establish an *affiliation* or *relationship* of any language under observation with a given linguistic continuum, there must be evidence of a common origin and unbroken transmission of linguistic symbols or features from a parent language to the language under observation. This is attested by Leonard Palmer (1972). In his text *Descriptive and Comparative Linguistics*, Palmer states:

> To trace the transmission of linguistic symbols is to write in part the history of the community which uses them. To reconstruct the ancestral forms which account for the resemblances in the communities under observation is simultaneously to make some kind of assertion about an ancestral community.... We repeat, then, that observed resemblances between speech habits, given the empirical principle of arbitrariness, force us to the conclusion of historical connectedness by an unbroken chain of mimetic acts. This connectedness is what is understood by 'relationship.' (Palmer, 1972: 22–23)

Thus, contend the Africologists, to reconstruct or trace the ancestral forms in any language or hybrid dialect to a given parent language family it must first and foremost be established that there is a *'common origin'* or *'genesis'* rooted in an identified *'common ancestor language.'* In order to do this a decision must be made as to which features in the language being observed and the identified ancestor language are the most reliable to establish a 'historical connectedness or relationship by an unbroken chain of mimetic acts.' That is, to establish a *'genetic kinship'* or *'relationship'* there must be evidence of a historical connectedness based on 'linguistic characteristics that are inherited by one generation of speakers from another, as opposed to those which are acquired from other sources' (Welmers, 1973: 3). Welmers clarifies the meaning of 'genesis' in his text, *African Language Structures*:

> Of course Greenberg and the body of scholars who generally share his theoretical bias never intended the word 'genetic' to be associated with 'genes' or 'genealogy'... it is associated rather with 'genesis' or origin, and 'genetic relationships' have to do with linguistic characteristics that are inherited by one generation of speakers from another, as opposed to those which are acquired from other sources.

According to the Africologists it is not the lexicon or mere points of vocabulary but continuity in the rules of 'grammar' that constitutes the relevant evidence for positing 'genetic relationship.' By this is meant, to establish a historical connectedness by an unbroken chain of mimetic acts or the linguistic characteristics that are inherited by one generation of speakers from another, as opposed to those acquired from other sources it is evidence of continuity in the rules of grammar that is regarded as being the most reliable. This is also confirmed by Leonard Palmer (1972: 23) who states, concerning historical connectedness or relationship in languages:

> In order to establish the fact of such a relationship our evidence must not consist entirely of points of vocabulary. For,... words are often borrowed by one language from another as a result of cultural contact. Thus, English has borrowed words like algebra from Arabic sources. No one on that account would state that English is genetically related to Arabic. What constitutes the most certain evidence of relationship is resemblance of grammatical structure, for languages retain their native structure even when their vocabularies have been swamped by foreign borrowings, such as has been the case of English and Hittite.

The Africologists posit that it is one thing to have a dispute over the specific criteria or features believed to be valid genetic classification. However, it is another to adhere to the same criteria to classify a language 'genetically' then to vacillate from those criteria to support a specious theory of genetic kinship based on vocabulary as opposed to grammar. As Mervyn Alleyne (1971: 125–126) states:

> The most prevalent view concerning the basis for genetic classification in Indo-European linguistics is that continuity of morphology constitutes the relevant evidence for positing genetic relationship. For example, there has been linguistic continuity in Western Europe in terms of the transmission of Latin morphology (in somewhat altered form) or by the transmission of old Germanic morphology. This makes languages like French, Spanish etc., genetically related to Latin, and German, Dutch, etc., genetically related to old Germanic. It is generally accepted that there has been no rupture in the development or transmission process, although obviously there has been change. English itself is considered to be a continuation of Anglo-Saxon and in turn of old Germanic, although in fact the vocabulary is predominantly Romance or Latin.

Affirming that it is common origin and continuity of the grammar that constitutes the relevant evidence for positing genetic kinship and that based on these criteria English is a Germanic language, noting also the East African language Swahili as being a notable example of extensive lexical borrowing, Welmers (1973: 7–8) states:

> English has borrowed vast numbers of words from French, but the phonology of English has been affected by French in only a few minor details, and the grammar even less. . . Swahili has experienced external influence to a degree that few languages ever do. In grammar, however, Swahili is unmistakably a Bantu language. No significant features of Arabic, English, or other foreign grammatical structures have crept into Swahili. A substantial part of modern English vocabulary has been borrowed from French, Latin, and Greek; a substantial though easily exaggerated part of modern Swahili vocabulary has been adopted from Arabic and English. But in structure, and in genetic relationship as reflected in regular phonetic correspondences in inherited vocabulary, English is still Germanic and Swahili is still Bantu.

As shown in the quotes of Alleyne and Welmers above in Indo-European linguistics, adherence to the principle that 'genetic classification' is based on a criteria of common origin or genesis and continuity of an identical grammatical pattern or rules of grammar presents no problem as a basis for genetic classification of Indo-European languages. Yet, for some strange and unexplained reason, some comparative linguists seem to have a major problem adhering to this principle as a basis for the genetic classification of African American speech. That is, when classifying Indo-European languages, the relevant evidence for positing genetic kinship is common origin and continuity of the morphosyntax. But when classifying African American speech, somehow despite the fact that Africans are from Africa and English people are from England, that is, different origins, the criteria becomes dominant parent lexifier and mutual intelligibility. We cannot look into the hearts and minds of those who take this inconsistent position, however, we can argue that their position supports the white cultural hegemonic position that continental African and African American people and by extension their language and culture deserve little or no equal human worth, social status and/or intellectual consideration.

The Africologists contend that, just as modern English was first a separate 'Anglish' dialect of German and yet, despite the extensive relexification that has occurred, English is still classified as being a

Germanic language. The Niger-Congo African languages of African Americans' ancestors have undergone a similar process. African American speech is the relexified morphosyntactical continuation of the West and Niger-Congo African linguistic tradition in African America.

The contention of the Africologists is that African American people were first introduced to the European English language during the historical period in which their autochthonous West and Niger-Congo African ancestors were being captured and enslaved by the ancestors of today's Euro-American English-speaking people. Hence, posit the Africologists, at the base of the historical process, African American speech has its origins in West and Niger-Congo Africa while the Euro-American's English has its origins in Anglo-Saxon Germany. According to the Africologists, the crux of the issue is, did a genetic shift occur as a result of the African and European linguistic convergence?

The view of the Africologists is that as a consequence of their being descendants of West and Niger-Congo African forebears, whose native languages were not English, to the extent that enslaved African descendants have historically been born into, reared in, and compelled to live in socially separate linguistic environments, (i.e. from Euro-American English-speaking people) African Americans have, in fact, retained a West and Niger-Congo African thought process. The Africologists contend that it is this African thought process that is dominant in the grammar of African American speech. But, because of the extensive lexical borrowing that has occurred, the African grammar is obscured and erroneously depicted as being a broken form of English.

The Africologists contend that since prior to any linguistic contact with Europeans, the native language of the ancestors of African American people was not 'genetically' the same as their European captors and to the extent that African Americans have retained an African deep phonetic, phonology, morphology, and syntax in their speech, the mother tongue or native language of African Americans is not 'genetically' European today. As Alleyne (1971: 126) states:

> If we find African elements in Afro-American dialects, the conclusion is inescapable that they belong to the base of the historical process. If we find an almost total absence of Indo-European morphology in Afro-American dialects, but instead find that the morphosyntax can in many respects be shown to be derived from the morphosyntax of West African languages, we can reasonably conclude that there is morphosyntactical continuity from West African languages to Afro-American dialects.

Some Africologists call the native language of African American people *Ebonics*. They explain that the term Ebonics is a compound of two words, 'Ebony' which means 'Black' and 'phonics' which means 'sounds,' – hence 'Black-Sounds' (Williams, 1975: vi). The Africologists contend that because Ebonics is not 'genetically' related to English, the term Ebonics is not a mere synonym for the more commonly used phrase 'Black English.'

In fact, posit the Africologists, according to Robert Williams, the psychologist who coined the term Ebonics, during a conference on the 'Cognitive and Language Development of the Black Child' in 1973, the consensus of the assembled Black scholars and his specific intent, when he coined the term Ebonics was in repudiation of the appellations Black English and nonstandard English. In his book *Ebonics: The True Language of Black Folks* (1975), Williams makes it clear that, after examining very critically the Euro-centric deficit versus difference models, the assembled Africologist Black scholars,

> . . . in a barrage of criticism, held that the concept of Black English or non-standard English contains deficit model characteristics, and therefore must be abolished. Following considerable discussion regarding the language of Black people, the group reached a consensus to adopt the term Ebonics (combining Ebony and phonics or Black sounds). (Williams, 1975: 100)

Clearly based on what the author of the term Ebonics states in the quote just above, the term Ebonics is not a synonym for the appellations Black English (BE), nonstandard English (NSE), Black Vernacular English (BVE), African American Vernacular English (AAVE), nonmainstream English (NME), or any other appellations or labels that assume tacitly that the language being discussed is a variety of English. Therefore, what is revealed is that those who use the term Ebonics as a synonym for BE, NSE, BVE, and AAVE etc., are utterly misinformed and lack the will or skills to research its origin and true meaning.

A critical analysis of the thesis that the native language of the descendants of enslaved West and Niger-Congo Africans in America is merely a dialect of English reveals that those who posit this view can be organized into two basis groups – those known as 'Pidgin/Creolists' in one group and those known as 'Generative Transformationalists or Dialectologists' in the other. In both of these groups there are some who do not deny the existence of African features in the speech of African Americans today. Yet in neither group is the speech of African Americans' native language viewed as an African dialect. In the pidgin/creolists group the thesis is that, while the creole or African English dialects spoken in the Caribbean and Latin America do indeed have African grammars in their substratum, AAE does *not*. In essence, unable to deny the West and Niger-Congo African origin of the African Americans' language, pidgin/creolists' thesis is that there was an African grammar divestment and English grammar adoption by African Americans. Therefore, being divested of all African grammatical features, the present-day native language of enslaved African descendants in America is entirely English, i.e. except for a scant few African words.

It is here that we have a crucial point of contention between the Africologists' view and pidgin/creole hypothesis. For, according to the Africologists, emanating from an African-centered paradigm, as defined by the Africologists, the term Ebonics refers not only to the language of US enslaved African descendants but to the dialects of enslaved African descendants in the Caribbean, South and Central American Diaspora as well. This is attested by Jahneinz Jahn (1961). In his work *Muntu: An Outline of the New African Culture*, Jahn concluded that throughout the Afro-American Diaspora the hybrid dialects that exist are the linguistic continuation of Africa. He states:

> In the Afro-American World some hybrid languages have arisen: Creole, Surinaams, Papiamento and others, which are generally designated as dialects. Creole counts as spoiled French. Surinaams is also called Negro-English. The vocabulary consists predominantly of European words, but the syntax and word formation follow the rules of African grammar. It is wrong therefore to call these languages 'spoilt' English or 'spoilt' French. If one considers the essence of a language to be its vocabulary, Creole and Papiamento must be called the youngest of the Romance languages; Surinaams must be called the youngest of the Germanic languages. But if one considers the grammatical structure of a language more important than its vocabulary, then the three languages mentioned do not belong to the Indo-European group. (Jahn, 1961: 194)

Thus, a critical analysis of the pidgin/creolists position reveals that when they contend that even though the hybrid dialects spoken by descendants of enslaved Africans in the Caribbean and Latin America have West and Niger-Congo African grammars, these dialects are still not African language *based*. At the crux of their dispute with the Africologists is that, as the term *'based'* is applied to hybrid languages that have African and European parents, the pidgin/creolists vacillate on what is meant by the term *based*. That is, the pidgin/creolists make an irrational shift from 'grammar' as their criterion for positing linguistic kinship and use instead the base from which the dominant lexicon is derived. In the case of AAE, the *base* is posited as the European 'superstrate' or 'English lexifier' parent. In her text *Language to Society*, Suzanne Romaine (1994) describes the pidgin/creolists' view of the term 'based' as the term is applied in pidgin/creole linguistics. She states:

> Pidgin and Creole language are spoken mainly in Third World countries...The exact number of languages is difficult to establish because it depends on how we define the terms 'pidgin' and 'creole.' Most pidgins and creoles are based on European languages, in particular Spanish, Portuguese, French, English and Dutch. However those based on English are more numerous than those based on any other language, attesting to the greater spread of English than any other metropolitan languages. The next largest group is based on French... The term 'based' means that the bulk of the lexicon is drawn from that language, while the grammatical structure typically shows influence from other (usually non-European) languages. These other languages are referred to as the 'substrate.' Thus when scholars speak of *English-based* creoles, they are referring to all those creoles that have taken most of their vocabulary from English. Terms such as 'English lexicon' or 'English lexifier' pidgin/creole are also used and the lexifier language is sometimes called the 'superstrate.' (Romaine, 1994: 163–164)

As stated earlier, in the 'Generative Transformationalists' or 'Dialectologists' group there are also some language scholars and researchers who do not deny the existence of African features in the speech of African Americans today. The Dialectologists are mostly in the fields of communications disorders, English literature, child psychology, sociology, and education. Like the pidgin/creolists, they reject the Africologists' idea that the descendants of enslaved Africans in America have 'retained' a Niger-Congo African grammar in the substratum of their hybrid language. The Dialectologists contend that the grammar rules that exist in the language of descendants of enslaved Africans in America are entirely derived from the NSE dialects of British settlers. In their view the West and Niger-Congo Africans who were captured and enslaved acquired a simplified English from their captors. This simplified English was then directly transmitted to the offspring of enslaved Niger-Congo Africans. The Dialectologists contend that being exposed only to this simplified English, over time the descendants of the enslaved West and

Niger-Congo Africans acquired this infantile English as their mother tongue (Ferguson, 1975; Krapp, 1924).

As for the African features that undeniably exist in the language of descendants of enslaved West and Niger-Congo Africans in America today, the Dialectologists contend that the enslaved Niger-Congo Africans in America retained little or no West and Niger-Congo African languages. This is precisely the view put forth by John McWhorter who states (1998: 11–12):

> African influence on Black English is light and indirect. Most nonstandard features in Black English are directly traceable not to Mende, Yoruba, or Kikongo but to regional dialects spoken by the British settlers whose English was what African slaves in America were exposed to... At best, African influence on Black English is largely restricted to intonation, some vocabulary items (most of them obsolete in urban culture) and patterns of social usage.

Thus, even though there are some non-Africologist language researchers and scholars who do acknowledge the existence of West and Niger-Congo African features in the speech of African Americans and Africans in the Caribbean and Latin American Diaspora today, most do not regard this as evidence that the language or dialects of descendants of enslaved Africans in Diaspora are neo-African dialects and languages. Instead they contrive all kinds of specious arguments to support the white cultural hegemonic thesis that the base from which the native language of African Americans derives is English. Ironically, the pidgin/creolists use grammar as their criterion to classify English as belonging to the Germanic language family and then vacillate from this criterion and use the parent language from which the bulk of the vocabulary or lexicon is derived to classify the language of descendants of enslaved Niger-Congo Africans as a BE dialect. The Generative Grammarians or Dialectologists contend that the grammar and the bulk of the vocabulary of the descendants of enslaved Africans' language is entirely derived from nonstandard British settler English and that even the African elements that can be found are not African retentions but rather are African features that were borrowed by the European settlers who then transmitted these African features to the enslaved Africans.

Contrarily, the Africologists see the base of AAE as West African Niger-Congo languages, using genesis classification as the means to present their argument. Thus, African American speech is the relexified morphosyntactical continuation of the West and Niger-Congo African linguistic tradition in America.

Here it should be made clear that just as some pidgin/creolists and Dialectologists have constructed specious arguments to deny that the native language of descendants of enslaved Africans in America belongs to the Niger-Congo African language system or family, they have been equal contributors in undermining and confusing the issue of Ebonics with which the Oakland Unified School District (OUSD) was confronted. By this is meant that in the district's home language surveys, the vast majority of parents of African American students identify English as the primary language spoken in their homes and as the language their child first learned. Therefore, the issue was not whether the language of African American pupils in the OUSD was a dialect of English or had become so different it was a separate language. The issue was, what is *Ebonics*? That is, if African American parents identify their child's home language as *Ebonics*, does the term *Ebonics* refer to an African language system or a dialect of English?

On December 18, 1996 in a unanimous vote the OUSD passed a resolution and adopted a policy declaring its finding that, based on the preponderance of the scholarly evidence presented to their Board, the term *Ebonics* as defined by its author, refers to an African language system. The OUSD adopted a policy that states in no uncertain terms that there is no double standard in the OUSD as to how languages are classified. In the OUSD there is a uniform criterion for the classifications of all languages and a mandate that all pupils are equal and that regardless of their race or national origin, all limited English proficient pupils are to be treated equally. On the issue of whether Ebonics refers to a dialect of English or an African language system, the policy adopted in the School District Board in Oakland California in December of 1996 states in part verbatim:

> There is persuasive empirical evidence that predicated on analysis of the phonology, morphology and syntax that currently exists as systematic, rule governed and predictable patterns in the grammar of African American speech... African Americans (1) have retained a West and Niger-Congo African linguistic structure in the substratum of their speech and (2) by this criteria are not native speakers of a Black dialect or any other dialect of English. Moreover, there is persuasive empirical evidence that, owing to their history as United States slave descendants of West and Niger-Congo origin, to the extent that African Americans have been born into, reared in, and continue to live in home environments that are different from the Euro-American English-speaking population, African American

people and their children, are from environments in which a language other than English is dominant.

Let us now consider the empirical evidence upon which the Africologists have based their thesis that Ebonics is a neo-African dialect or language derived directly from the West and Niger-Congo African languages of the African Americans' enslaved ancestors. First however, it should be noted that in keeping with the comparative linguistic principle that to establish genetic kinship there must be a common origin in the unbroken historical connectedness to a specified common ancestor language, it was Lorenzo Dow Turner who was the first to scientifically counter the argument that there was no provable African content surviving in African American speech. In his work *Africanism in the Gullah Dialect* (1974), Turner describes how in their Eurocentric refusal to acquaint themselves with the West African languages from which the enslaved Africans were brought, European scholars 'greatly underestimated the extent of the African element in Gullah.' Turner (1974: 5) states:

> Observing many characteristics that Gullah has in common with certain British dialects of the seventeenth and eighteenth centuries, they have not considered it necessary to acquaint themselves with any of the languages spoken in those sections of West Africa from which the Negroes were brought to the New World as slaves, nor to study the speech of the Negroes in those parts of the New World where English is not spoken; but rather have they taken the position that the British dialects offer a satisfactory solution to all the problems presented by Gullah.

Turner's rare piece of scholarship challenged the White academic linguistic establishment's theory that the clash between the traditional African and the colonial European cultures resulted in a subculture of 'Black Europeans.' Turner was able not only to identify the specific African linguistic features surviving in African American speech (Gullah); he also provided a list of the precise ethnic groups and language specific dialects from which these features are derived. Turner (1974: 1) writes:

> The slaves brought to South Carolina and Georgia direct from Africa came principally from a section along the West Coast extending from Senegal to Angola. The important areas involved were Senegal, Gambia, Sierra Leone, Liberia, the Gold Coast, Togo, Dahomey, Nigeria, and Angola. Today the vocabulary of Gullah contains words

found in the following languages, all of which are spoken in the above-mentioned areas: Wolof, Malinke, Mandinka, Bambara, Fula, Mende, Vai, Twi, Fante, Ga, Ewe, Fon, Yoruba, Bini, Hausa, Ibo, Ibibio, Efik, Kongo, Umbundu, Kimbundu, and a few others.

The Africologists contend that the ethnic-specific African dialects and languages listed above were structurally different from the European languages of the colonists. By this is meant, the rules for combining the sounds to shape and form words (the morphology) and the rules for arranging words to express a complete thought (the syntax) were different. According to the Africologists, based on these criteria, despite the blending that has occurred, Afro-American and Euro-American speech were not originally the same and they are not genetically related today.

When Africologists contend that the grammar rules of Ebonics follows the grammar rules distinctive of the Niger-Congo African languages they often rely on and cite the works of many European and Euro-American Africanists whose works are generally regarded as authentic and reliable. They maintain that the African grammatical features described by the Africanists are traits that these authors have observed. Therefore, if what the Africanists describe does not exist or is inaccurately reported, then it is the Africanists' research which should be criticized and rejected and not that of the Africologists. The Africologists have merely demonstrated that in AAE the same grammatical features and rules, described by the Africanists, still exist today and that as originally Niger-Congo African features, there is a historical connectedness by an unbroken chain of mimetic acts. In his text, *African Languages Structures*, William Wehners (1973) states:

> In many Niger-Congo languages... nasalization in exclusively final position may often be analyzed as a final nasal, ordinarily /n/ or /ŋ/. This can be done in the Senufo languages, Bambara, Ewe, and Yoruba with no difficulty (p. 33). No language seems to have doubly articulated stops in syllable final position (p. 48). In Nilo Saharan as well as in Niger-Congo consonant clusters are generally rare (p. 53). In many languages there is a single construction which has explicit and exclusive reference to past action; for such languages it is quite legitimate to speak of a 'past' construction... On the other hand, there are a number of languages which have more than one construction referring to past time. Some Bantu languages distinguish a 'near past' (particularly with reference to action performed earlier on the same day) and a 'remote past'. (p. 348)

Peter Ladefoged (1968) conducted an extensive study of the consonant structure of West African languages. In his work *A Phonetic Study of West African Languages*, describing the Kwa group, Ladefoged (1968: 1) states:

> Many West African languages, including most of the Kwa group, can be considered to have no consonant clusters. . . I have tried to include in Table I all the contrasting consonants in at least those languages that have a simple CV structure.

In his text, *Yoruba*, E.C. Rowlands (1979: 9), describes the syllable structure of Yoruba as follows:

> A syllable in Yoruba may have one of three forms; it may be a vowel, a consonant plus a vowel, or a nasal (written m or n). It is not possible to have groups of consonants in any position or to have syllables ending in consonants.

According to Victoria Fromkin and Robert Rodman (1975) in their text, *An Introduction to Language*, English and Twi, a West African language, are from distinctly different language families. Comparing the phonetic inventories of this Germanic and West African language, they state:

> Consider for example, English and Twi, two widely different languages from two distinct language families. They both contain the consonants /p/, /t/, /k/, /b/, /d/, /g/, /m/, /n/, /ŋ/, /f/, /s/, /h/, /r/, /w/, /y/, /č/, /ǰ/ and the vowels /i/, /I/, /e/, /ɛ /, /u/, / ʊ/, / ɔ/, and /a/. There are sounds in English not found in Twi, such as /z/, /v/, /θ/, /ð/and /l/. (Fromkin & Rodman, 1975: 227)

Notice that in Twi the /f/ exists but that the voiceless and voiced -th /θ/ and /ð/ do not.

According to Ayo Banjo (1974: 36) in his work *Sentence Negation in Yoruba and Hausa*, there is no verb to indicate 'present tense' as such. The marker that indicates is/was can actually be used to indicate two notions of time: the progressive and the habitual. He states:

> We could have said 'Ade is/was in the habit of singing.' The reason for this is that the continuous marker can be used in the language to express both the progressive and the habitual.

Charles Kraft and A.H.M. Kirk-Greene (1979: 36– 37) describe the verb system and syntactic structure of Hausa, a Niger-Congo African language. In their text Hausa they state:

In Hausa the aspect (termed aspect rather than tense since it denotes kind of action rather than time of action) of verbs is shown by changes in the person aspect pronoun not in the verb itself. This precedes the verb... In every aspect in Hausa, except the imperative, the verb must, unlike English, be preceded by a person aspect pronoun (hence forth abbreviated p-a or pa-a pronoun), regardless whether there is already a noun subject or not. Examples:

Audu ya zo.	Audu (he) come.
Yara sun tafi.	The boys (they) gone.

Kraft and Kirk-Green (1979: 36) also report that because the verb system of Hausa is aspectual and not tense there are several other aspects. One of these is the aspect of 'completion,' which has two forms. They state:

> The completion aspect indicates action regarded as complete or as occurring at a specific point (rather than as a process) in time. This point may be past, present or future as indicated by the context... There are two forms of the completive aspect.

Having examined the grammar of autochthonous or continental Niger-Congo African languages, based upon what Welmers, Ladefoged, Rowlands, Fromkin and Rodman, Banjo, Kraft and Kirk-Greene have posited here, in the West and Niger-Congo African languages there are few instances, if any, in which consonant cluster configurations and consonants in coda exist (by coda it is meant the syllable or word final position). Also based upon what Welmers, Ladefoged and Rowlands have stated, in the West and Niger-Congo African languages the syllable structure is strongly a consonant vowel, that is, CV vocalic pattern. Ayo Banjo explains the aspect of progression and habitual time in Yoruba and Kraft and Kirk-Greene's description of Hausa provides an example of the 'topic' and 'comment' phrase structure in which the 'person aspect' or 'recapitulative pronoun' occurs in the comment segment of the sentence. They also generally explain the aspect of completion in Hausa. Welmers describes the notion of aspect of remote time that generally exists in most African languages. Let us examine now the grammar that exists in the substratum of AAE. For the Africologists maintain that the grammar of Ebonics originated in and even today still follows the grammar rules of the Niger-Congo African languages.

The Africologists contend that, as has been shown above, the West and Niger-Congo African languages did not originally contain certain consonant cluster configurations. Therefore, the Africologists maintain that, if African American speech does not contain these consonant cluster configurations or consonants in coda today, the same phonotactic restrictions in Ebonics today is a linguistic continuation of the phonological rules of the original West and Niger-Congo African languages.

For example, Key *et al*. (1971) discerned a strong consonant–vowel (CV) pattern in the shape of the syllable in African American speech. While the aim of the study by Key *et al*. was not diachronic or comparative, the assumption of a genetic kinship with English notwithstanding, the Key *et al*. study provides empirical data on the deep phonetic, phonological, and morphosyntactical structure of African American speech. Key *et al*. (1971: 187) state:

> The canonical form (or shape) of the syllable in BE is strongly a consonant–vowel (CV) pattern. Previous studies have described the deletion of final consonants such as the stops and /1/ and /r/ and the reduction of final clusters such as /-st, -ft, -kt, -ld/ to a single consonant. When a syllable does end in a consonant there is a tendency for the consonant to carry over and begin the next syllable. For example, 'get a look' syllabically divided into /ge.ta.look/; 'all the' /a.le/; 'cause I' /k.zai/; 'down there' /dau.ner/; 'than that' /den.nat/ or /de.nat/; 'trying to' /trai.na/.

Thus, contend the Africologists, in the deep phonology of African American speech there is a distinctively West and Niger-Congo African CV (consonant vowel) vocalic pattern that has been retained. As a result of having retained this CV rule, in the deep phonology of African American speech, in consonance with the rules of the West and Niger-Congo African languages, certain consonant clusters or consonant blends do not occur.

According to the Africologists, most researchers who have studied African American speech have noted that word final consonant clusters are phonotactically restricted. But, as Key *et al*. have stated in the quote above, these studies have negatively and incorrectly described the absence of consonants in coda as being a deletion of final consonants or their 'reduction to a single consonant.' Using terms like: 'weakened,' 'dropped,' 'deleted,' 'lost,' 'simplified,' 'omitted,' or 'reduced' (Baratz, 1969; Burling, 1973; Fasold, 1973; Labov, 1975; Stoller, 1975; Thomas, 1973; Welty, 1971; Wolfram, 1973) have thus depicted African American speech as being a pathological, disordered, handicapped, substandard, impoverished, deprived, disadvantaged, deficient, deviant and dysfunctional lazy speech.

Following this study of the CV structure in the deep phonology of African American speech, Smith continued research to show that African American speech was not a Black dialect of English (1978, 1994, 1995, 1997). Smith and other Africologists contend that in AAE there is no weakening, deletion, omission, loss, or reduction of anything. Firstly, in consonance with the phonological rules of the West and Niger-Congo African languages, certain consonant clusters never even existed. Secondly, and likewise in consonance with the phonological rules of Niger-Congo African grammar, it is primarily the homogenous consonant blends or consonant cluster configurations that tend not to occur in African American speech. With only one or two exceptions, in the case of heterogeneous final consonant clusters, (i.e. when one consonant member is voiced and the other is voiceless) such clusters are quite the norm. Therefore, it would be erroneous to say that word final consonant clusters do not exist in African or AAE at all.

Thus, as a rule in AAE, homogeneous consonant clusters tend not to occur. This is not because the final phoneme has been 'lost,' 'reduced,' 'weakened,' 'simplified,' 'deleted,' or 'omitted,' but because it never existed in the first place. It is then by relexification that in AAE, the English words 'west,' 'best,' 'test,' 'last,' and 'fast' become 'wes,' 'bes,' 'tes,' 'las' and 'fas;' the words 'land,' 'band,' 'sand,' and 'hand' become 'lan,' 'ban,' 'san,' and 'han;' and 'left,' 'lift,' 'drift' and 'swift' become 'lef,' 'lif,' 'drif,' and 'swif;' and so forth.

Similarly, because the canonical form or shape of syllable structure of AAE is that of the Niger-Congo African languages [i.e. strongly a consonant vowel, consonant vowel (CV) vocalic pattern] by relexification in Ebonics, entire sentences will have a CV vocalic pattern. Thus, in AAE, a sentence such as 'did you eat yet?' will exhibit the CVCV vocalic pattern /ĵiĵɛt/ or /ĵuwiĵɛt/. The reply 'No, or naw did you?' will exhibit the CV vocalic pattern /n) ju/. The sentence 'did you eat your jello?' will by relexification exhibit the CV pattern /ĵ u w í č o ĵ ɛ l o/.

Because some scholars view African American speech as being an English dialect, they contend that in sentences such as 'You the man' and 'That girl she nice,' a copula verbal or the verb 'to be' has been 'deleted,' 'dropped,' or 'omitted.' In contrast, because Africologists view the language of African descendants as an African language system, the Africologists contend that in the sentences 'You the man' and 'That girl she nice' there has been no 'deleted,' 'dropped,' or 'omitted' copula or verb 'to be.' As an African language system that has an equational or equative clause phrase structure, the verb 'to be' never existed in the first place.

Absolutely convinced that AAE is a vernacular dialect of English, some scholars have also posited the existence of 'double subjects' in so-called BE. Because they view AAE as being an English dialect, some scholars mistakenly divide sentences such as 'That girl she nice' and 'My sister she smart' into noun phrase (NP) and verb phrase (VP) constituents – as English would be properly divided. In contrast, the Africologists, equally convinced that AAE is in fact an African linguistic system, do not divide sentences such as 'That girl she nice' and 'My sister she smart' into NP and VP constituents. As an African language system, the division of an equative clause sentence structure is into 'topic and comment' constituents. Hence, the pronoun 'she' that follows the common nouns 'girl' and 'sister' in each sentence is not a constituent of the 'topic' segment of the sentence. It is a recapitulative or person aspect pronoun that belongs to the 'comment' segment or portion of the sentence.

Thus, we have examined here a few specific grammatical features of AAE that distinguishes it as being the linguistic continuation of Africa in African America. The focus of this work being limited to an explanation of the Africologist ethnolinguistic theory on the historical development of African American speech, the aim of the foregoing discussion has been merely to provide a concrete example of what the Africologists view as being deep structure linguistic retentions of the West and Niger-Congo African languages. There is a substantial body of literature that contains many correct and factual observations and descriptions of African language structures. In our view, if there is a sincere desire to discern it, identifying the structural linguistic features in African American speech that remain as provable African content, is not difficult at all. As Winifred Kellersberger Vass (1979: 27) very aptly states in her work, *The Bantu Speaking Heritage of the United States*, 'Actually there is no lack of provable African content. There is simply a lack of those able to identify it.'

Now we will discuss the educational implications of AAE and the special language needs of AAE-speaking students who attend public schools where SAE is the language of instruction.

English Language Instruction for African American Ebonics Speakers

The Africologists' view of the historical origins of AAE defines and describes the language of many African American students attending school today. These students attend public and private schools where SAE is the language of instruction. The question now becomes what specific instructional prescriptions and practices would best support the acquisition of English for those students. Given our view that the grammars of AAE and SAE, or more precisely 'academic English', are different not only in a variety of surface features but more importantly in the deep structure, we believe English language instruction is appropriate for AAE-speaking students. Teaching English Language Arts as a second language incorporates best teaching practices that will meet the linguistic and cultural needs of African American students who speak AAE.

Moreover, the challenge of facilitating the development of bilingual African American students whose first language is Ebonics in a context where the language of instruction is English cannot be simply discussed in terms of bilingualism. More importantly it must be discussed in terms of biliteracy. For in a truly multicultural society where diversity is not only acknowledged but also embraced, AAE-speaking public school students and families must be given the option of preserving their first language while adding a second. They should not be forced to erase their first language to acquire a second one. Nor should English language learners (ELLs) be required to speak English fluently before gaining access to the public school curriculum.

The position advanced here is that AAE-speaking students need to learn how to read and write proficiently in Standard English or academic English in order to have continued and complete access to and educational success in public and private schools. Yet the two processes are interrelated and affect each other while occurring simultaneously. That is to say, while students develop their literacy skills in Standard English they gain greater access to the curriculum. This access to the curriculum reinforces and supports their literacy development.

As stated above, the stress must be on the development of biliterates. Second language instruction for AAE-speaking students must help students transfer and translate the deep structure of language of their first language into the deep structure of the new language they are acquiring, i.e. Standard English.

Language and literacy are inseparable. In fact and in practice language is the foundation for literacy development. Furthermore, as Cummins argues, students' first language can be used as the foundation for language and literacy development in a second language. The case in point is that the language and literacy development of AAE speakers in public schools must begin with their language, Ebonics. Educators greeting AAE-speaking students must first recognize that the language students bring is an important part of the student's and his/her family and community's identity. At the same time educators must recognize that students should be welcomed from not only this collective communal and cultural base but also as individuals who are living examples of the synthesis of historical and contemporary African and American experiences. That is, to say that although we recognize that many if not most African Americans speak AAE, we cannot at the same time say those who do use the same linguistic features all the time. Nor can we say that they have the same lived-experiences as a result of those shared experiences or the same instructional level of entry for acquisition of English. Nonetheless, there is a common thread which links and reflects a collective consciousness, condition and life-chances shared by many African American people in general and students specifically.

An effective methodology for ELLs is to use students' language and culture as an instructional 'jumping off' and/or sociological 'centering point' from which literacy is developed. This instructional approach views students' personal and communal capital as assets for the educational project. Students' personal strengths and weaknesses are assessed to indicate baselines for development along the continuum in language and literacy development. Literacy in this sense is viewed as the ability to engage the world in thought, in what is heard, in what is spoken, and what is written.

Student-centered Approach to English Language Learning – Additive Bilingualism

Given this educational project is rooted in the larger human project of socializing children in the values and views of the society, effective instruction for African American learners who are also ELLs reflects African American sensibilities, acknowledges the historical origins of AAE, sees literacy development for ELLs not as a linear process but as a continuum where students interact within concentric circles of family, ethnicity, age, gender, and school cultures. As such, the approach advanced here is based on several constructs.

These constructs outline important attitudinal traits and practices of effective teachers of African American learners. A central construct is a principle of practice that stresses quality relationships. It is that 'a person is a person through other people.' For it is in relationships – parent to child, teacher to student, sister to brother, friend to friend – that good, beautiful, knowledgeable and productive people are brought into being. Tied closely to this tenet is the belief and commitment to respect the child as a full human personality as well as human potentiality, valuing children's rich experiences and abilities while attending to the needs of the whole child. A third important construct recognizes the area of educational foundations in child sociology and psychology. As such, practitioners are encouraged to build their instruction around child development stages that outline expectations and approximations of cognitive and social development for children of varying age levels and groupings. A fourth construct offers a methodology of instruction based on viewing the child as a human with personal needs and as such, the instructional approach must begin with an assessment of each student's strengths and needs. Moreover, they see the results of this assessment as a beginning point for the instructional process, not an indictment of the child or validation for a less than rigorous, comprehensive curriculum. This approach is not *the lump, generalize, and dump* approach that diminishes and confuses human diversity and richness. Contrarily, it recognizes the reality of each student as a unique person who resides and relates within the context of a unique community and culture while valuing her/his opportunity to contribute to the on-going human development project.

The strategies discussed here are based on the research of several education scholars, including but not limited to: Janice Hale (1982), Michele Foster (1997), Wade Boykins (1996), Jim Cummins (1990), Steven Krashen (1982), Maulana Karenga (1994), Jacob Carruthers (1997), Asa Hilliard (1995), Jacqueline, and Martine Brooks (1993), and a number of practitioners, including myself and colleagues in the Los Angeles Unified School District's Language Development Program for African American Students (currently called American English Mastery Program) and the Mary McLeod Bethune Institute in Los Angeles. These researchers and practitioners have studied and implemented effective teaching strategies for African American students and/or the general student population. Boykins (1985) argues that a 'familiar cultural context of "verve"' – which includes cooperative groups where students are encouraged to develop interdependent relations, provisions of learning environments that incorporate movement and free, independent activity, introduction of subject matter with active content – reinforces and builds on the cultural base students bring with them.

Janice Hale (1982) supports Boykins view and argues that effective teaching should not only include Black culture but gender- and age-appropriate cultural materials and strategies. Michele Foster (1997), in her study of Afrocentric schools in San Francisco, documented several aspects of effective classrooms and instruction. They include: the display of visuals that are Afrocentric, everyday predictable rituals, African American curricular content incorporated throughout the curriculum, situational enactment (the use of classical cultural ethics as a method of classroom management, i.e. doing maat, incorporating things that are good for Black children, i.e. rhyme, rhythm, repetition, and movement, and things that are good for all children, i.e. student-centered activities.

Jacqueline and Martin Brooks (1993) argue for a shift in pedagogical paradigms where children's knowledge and experiences are acknowledged and valued rather then dismissed. They argue for student-initiated questions and student-to-student interactions to become the norm. As such, the strategies suggested here are based on the assumption that students enter the educational project with varying experiences and skills; they are not empty cups waiting to be filled but rather flower bulbs anticipating the right environment and support to blossom.

Jim Cummins (1990) argues that an effective language acquisition pedagogy for ELLs rests within a Pedagogy of Empowerment where the teacher facilitates the student becoming the center and master of his/her own education. In so doing, teachers give their students a sense of control over their lives and students develop confidence, ability, and motivation to achieve (Cummins, 1990). Such a pedagogy starts with an introduction of the significance of language instruction for all students and, more importantly, for English learning students. This includes a discussion of the relationship of language to students' academic achievement, in that communicative competence affects their ability to profit from the teaching and learning process. This pedagogy views language acquisition as a complex issue that involves not only methodology but also requires practitioners to have a comprehensive grasp of language development and linguistics, stressing how humans in general and children in particular acquire their first and subsequent languages, and the similarities and differences between these two processes. Contextualization of the language issue within the socio-political arena which informs and establishes language policy for schools, instructional practices of second language teachers, and the resulting implications of such policy on second language learners is a beginning point for this theoretical framework.

Two major school language policy approaches are Subtractive and Additive Bilingualism, with each offering different approaches, principles, and goals relating to the instruction of ELLs. The approaches to English language instruction under a framework of Subtractive Bilingualism generally develop from the deficit perspective where proponents believe the first language of ELLs inhibits their acquisition of English. As such, the first language is given a lower status than English. This approach generally seeks to maintain the status quo while disregarding the differences in language and culture of various groups in America. This approach does not recognize that differences enrich American culture rather than undermine it, and that a strong unified America need not and will not be created by denying differences. Even if all were committed to a common language for all Americans the process is not an easy one, for it normally takes five to seven years to develop fluency in a second language. This approach also usually focuses on oral production of the new language exclusively rather than the comprehensive and complex aspects of language in terms of listening, speaking, writing, and reading. When ELLs acquire some level of oral fluency the subtractive bilingual approach generally assumes students know the rules of the target language in all of the areas of language. If these students do not acquire English proficiency, their limited English is sometimes misread as limited cognitive ability. This scenario too often occurs with African American student populations where a disproportionate number of African American students are placed in special education classes (Heller *et al.*, 1982).

An alternative and more effective methodology is Additive Bilingualism, which incorporates the following components: effective second language acquisition instruction develops from the multiple perspectives position (Cheng, 1997) which respects students' first language and culture, acknowledging the first language as a complete, systematic linguistic system with rules for forming sounds, words, sentences, and nonverbal elements. There is also recognition that students have mastered, in most instances, their first language and have communicative competence in it. Students' first language is not viewed as a deficit but rather as one of many human languages full of rich experiences from which to build and expand other experiences and competencies. Moreover, educators' integration of the culture and language of the child into all subjects helps culturally to ground and support students' cognitive as well as affective domains (Hoover, 1994; Karenga, 1994).

Teachers who employ this methodology understand how language develops normally and naturally (students can learn in any language and learning is transferable.) Therefore, practitioners make a distinction between language difference and cognitive ability, yet understand the connection between the two languages is thought. Thinking and understanding must take place if cognitive development is to occur. Teachers also show an appreciation and respect for diversity. Human diversity, or language diversity is human richness – knowing the diverse presentations of humans through languages and cultures enriches one's life (Karenga, 1994). Thus practitioners acquire a knowledge of the linguistic features of the student's first language – phonics, phonology, morphology, syntax, and semantics, thereby recognizing, in the case of AAE, that West and Niger-Congo linguistic structure has been retained not only in the speech but the deep thought (grammar) of African American students. Also, the target language, as well as the similarities and differences between the two languages – that is, the rules of second language – are taught (Delpit, 1995). Effective second language methodology recognizes the rich experiences students bring to the educational project and the effect this inclusion has on empowering students.

The following describes optimum teacher behaviors:

- develops instructional practices from the difference perspective rather than the deficit perspective;
- understands how language develops normally/naturally;
- appreciates and respects diversity;
- sees first language as foundation on which to develop second;
- gains familiarity with linguistic features of AAE;
- gains familiarity with culture of students; understands the unity and diversity within and out of the culture;
- takes responsibility for facilitating acquisition of second language; sees the importance of empowering students in their education;
- recognizes the rich experiences students bring to the educational project;
- understands and appreciates the demands of acquiring a second language – hard work and long struggle (5–7 years);
- does not introduce disembodied knowledge (Dubois); uses culture of child to teach all subjects;
- understands that the success or failure in second language/literacy acquisition affects all subjects.

A critical component of such a language methodology is a presentation of African American Language, that is, Ebonics, and its effect on literacy skills of African American ELLs. Methodologies proven effective with African American student populations are demonstrated. This approach begins with the statistical reality that possibly as many as 85–90% (Smitherman, 1974), or at least 60% (Labov, 1975Labov, 1985) of African American people speak some or many aspects of Ebonics. Moreover, when African American children enter public schools they are met with a different linguistic and cultural system which needs to be introduced and taught to them. As such, AAE-speaking students are in practice ELLs who need English language instruction.

What does this instruction for African American ELLs look like? There are varying models, however, key aspects of these models include these principles: (a) language drives curriculum, in those circumstances where English is the language of instruction, practitioners acknowledge and use instructional practices that identify and teach differences in AAE and English; and (b) this language instruction does not focus exclusively on speech but rather sees language acquisition in English as communicative competence in listening/speaking, reading, and writing. An outline of these components follows:

- The learning community provides English-speaking models, and lots of stress-free practice (dialogues, debates, presentations).
- The learning community reduces affective filters: eliminates anxiety (doesn't correct by humiliation, reinforces strong self-concept, promotes internal motivation) (Krashen, 1982).
- The learning community provides comprehensible input (visuals, graphic organizers, adapts language) (Cummins, 1989).

Reading and Writing With Second Language Learners

Reading and writing as complex, academic skills are best taught in the context of real-life experiences. A balanced whole language approach employing language experience activities has been an effective, personalized tool for ELLs. This approach recognizes and respects the vast and rich background that ELLs bring with them to the classroom and draws on prior experiences to provide new meaningful experiences while showing similarities and differences between the two languages and cultures. As such, the teacher facilitates critical and creative thinking, reading and writing about one's personal life as well as the life of others in the learning community in both the first and second language. The point of departure rests in young learners' need to start with concrete, familiar experiences then move to and through the pictorial to the abstract. The focus is on making meaning by setting up learning environments that build understanding and knowledge in particular areas then link the abstract to the concrete experience. This is not just good practice for young learners but older learners as well – those who have not had the opportunity and instructional support to develop reading and writing fluency in their first and/or second language. Moreover, for learning to occur there must first be understanding – meaning needs to exist in the minds and hearts of the learner before true literacy or biliteracy can develop. Effective teachers of ELLs reject the notion that there is linguistic interference when Ebonics speakers read English text because they stress the importance of extracting meaning from the text and building understanding and connections.

> More attention should be devoted to the difference between receptive and productive language processes, and the competence needed to use them effectively. As reading is a receptive process, a reader does not need to be able to speak a dialect in order to read it... analysis of a group of second graders who were reading some of the dialect-specific materials and companion stories in SE revealed that, while the dialect did not cause any difficulty for the children, neither did it enhance the process, nor did it eliminate any problems which may have occurred in the reading of SE... in the final analysis, much of what happens in language teaching is determined by the skills and abilities of teachers... if teachers believe that their students are deficient in cognitive or language skills, that belief will be reflected in their teaching and in their students' lack of achievement. (Sims, 1975)

Effective practitioners start where the students are and take them to where they would like them to be by using the language and culture children bring to school as a foundation upon which to build. Careful attention is placed on eradicating the negative value connotation that the schools and society have placed on Black Vernacular (Simpkins, 1997). Many use African American literature, which has cultural and linguistic experiences of children, for example, Lucille Clifton's *My Brother Fine With Me* and June Jordon's story of *Fannie Lou Hamer*.

Using process writing is problematic for ELLs (Whimbey, 1995), therefore, use this method while employing a number of reinforcing writing strategies. Whimbey's sentence combining and text reconstruction activities have been used effectively with African American ELLs. These activities help learners develop their ability to expand simple sentences into complex ideas and concepts as well as extend their understanding of the logic and sequence in paragraphing. Another strategy introduces and reinforces the rules of the target language/culture (Delpit, 1996). This strategy should not be used under the assumption that all African American ELLs are clueless about the same rules. Rather practitioners should observe and assess learners on an individual bases. What is required here is that the teacher and student develop a list of personalized editing notes and rules based on the individual writings of a learner as opposed to a blanket approach covering all of the rules and common errors in the English language. Students then use these notes and rules as references when writing. More importantly, students should also be given the opportunity to play with deeper meanings, thoughts, logic in the language (sentence combining, text reconstruction, analogies, alliteration, complex/descriptive meanings), as opposed to simply the surface features of English.

Effective language instruction must consider cultural learning approaches of the target population. As Boykins (1985) argued above, a familiar, supportive cultural context is important for African American students' educational success. While we encourage teachers to provide familiar, supportive environments for learners, we also encourage the provision of activities and discussions to dispel myths and negativism about students' culture and socioeconomic background. In an attempt to counter the negative effects of racism and classism in schools, effective practitioners recognize that students of color and poverty receive the least attention to how they can learn. Their socioeconomic status and race, rather than effective instructional practices, often dictate their treatment

> Race, minority status, socioeconomic status, and other variables are not factors that predict what students can learn. More likely than not, they predict how schools will treat children. (Hilliard, 1995: xiv)

Therefore, second language instruction includes a curriculum of culture that integrates history and present-day realities designed to complement and support the academic achievement of students. Culture in its fullest sense means the personal and collective experiences students create and/or witness while reflecting and interacting in the home, the school, the community, and the larger society. Let us consider for a moment the culture of African American students. Afrocentrists contend that with a critical understanding of culture and accompanying instructional practices, educators will be able to overturn student outcomes, encourage greater social responsibility, and expand students' positive self-conception to include positive images of their people (Karenga, 1995).

For example, proponents of African-centered curricula have long recognized the necessity of using materials to counter the negative images of African people in the minds of students and the larger society. While students' self-conception is generally positive, their image of African and diasporan African people as a whole is generally negative (Carruthers, 1997). Therefore, cultural workshops for teachers, administrators, parents, and paraprofessionals should focus on the affective needs of African American students. These presentations may include a survey of history and current events that portrays the strengths, contributions, and achievements of historic and contemporary African American people.

The activities suggested above are by no means exhaustive; they are merely a brief overview of some practices that have worked with African American children of varying language needs and academic abilities. One must remember that all African American children are not the same and a multiplicity of activities should be used to meet the needs and goals established for the specific individual and groups in the target population. Our major concern in this article, however, was to demonstrate that ineffective, limited educational practices have been used with African American students based on the erroneous position that many speak an English dialect rather than, as we have argued, an African dialect. It is our hope that this African-centered position will better focus and direct the educational needs of our children where their potential is fully realized.

References

Alleyne, M.C. (1971) Linguistic continuity of Africa in the Caribbean. In H.J. Richards (ed.) *Topics in Afro-American Studies* (pp. 119–134). New York: Black Academy Press.

Ambrose-Grillet, J. (1978) *Glossary of Transformational Grammar*. Rowley, MA: Newbury House Publishers, Inc.

Auerbach, J., Cook, E.H., Kaplan, R.B. and Tufte, V.J. (1968) *Transformational Grammar: A Guide for Teachers*. Rockville, MD: English Language Services.

Bailey, B.L. (1977) Jamaican Creole. In D. Hymes (ed.) *Pidginization and Creolization of Languages* (pp. 341–348). New York: Cambridge University Press.

Banjo, A. (1974) *Sentence Negation in Yoruba*. Los Angeles: Studies in African Linguistics.

Baratz, J. (1970) Educational considerations for teaching standard English to Negro children. In R.W. Fasold and R.W. Shuy (eds) *Teaching Standard English in the Inner City* (pp. 20–40). Washington, DC: The Center for Applied Linguistics.

Blackshire-Belay, A.C. (1996) The location of Ebonics within the framework of the Africological paradigm. *Journal of Black Studies* 27, 5–23.

Bornstein, D.D. (1977) *An Introduction to Transformational Grammar*. Cambridge, MA: Winthrop Publishers, Inc.

Boykins, A.W. and Toms, F.D. (1985) Black child socialization. In H.P. McAdoo and J.L. McAdoo (eds) *Black Children: Social Educational, and Parental Environments* (pp. 33–51). Beverly Hills, CA: Sage.

Brooks, J.G. and Brooks, M.G. (1993) *In Search of Understanding: The Case for Constructivist Classrooms*. Alexandria, VA: Association for Supervision and Curriculum Development.

Carruthers, J. (1995) African-centered education. http://www.nbufront.org/html/FrontalView/ArticlesPapers/jake1.html

Cheng, L. (1997) Diversity: Challenges and implications for assessment. *Journal of Children's Communication Development* 19 (1), 53–61.

Chomsky, N. (1972) *Language and Mind*. New York: Harcourt Brace Janovich, Inc.

Cummins, J. (1989) *Empowering Minority Students*. Sacramento, CA: California Association for Bilingual Education.

De Camp, D. (1977) Introduction: The study of pidgin and creole languages. In D. Hymes (ed.) *Pidginization and Creolization of Languages* (pp. 13–39). New York: Cambridge University Press.

Delpit, L. (1995) *Other People's Children: Cultural Conflict in the Classroom*. New York: The New Press.

Dillard, J.L. (1972) *Black English. Its History and Usage in the United States*. New York: Vintage Books.

Fasold, R.W. and Wolfram, W. (1970) Some linguistic features of Negro dialect. In R.W. Fasold and R.W. Shuy (eds) *Teaching Standard English in the Inner City* (pp. 41–86). Washington, DC: The Center for Applied Linguistics.

Ferguson, C. (1975) Toward a characterization of English as foreigner talk. *Anthropological Linguistics* 17, 1–14.

Fishman, J. (1975) *Sociolinguistics: A Brief Introduction*. Rowley, MA. Newbury House Language Series.

Foster, M. (1997) Ethnographic research – Study of Afrocentric schools in San Francisco – classnotes. Claremont Graduate University.

Fromkin, V. and Rodman, R. (1993) *An Introduction to Language*. New York: Holt Rinehart and Winston.

Gonzales, A.E. (1922) *The Black Border: Gullah, Stories of the Carolina Coast*. Columbia, SC: The State Company.

Greenberg, J.H. (1966) *Essays in Linguistics*. Chicago: University of Chicago Press.

Hall, R.A. Jr. (1962) The life cycle of languages. *Lingua* 11, 152–156.

Harris, R.A. (1993) *The Linguistic Wars*. New York: Oxford University Press.

Hartmann, R.R.K. and Stork, E.C. (1976) *Dictionary of Language and Linguistics*. New York: John Wiley & Sons.

Heller, K.A., Holtzman, W.H. and Messick, S. (eds) (1982) *Placing Children in Special Education: A Strategy for Equity*. Washington, DC: National Academic Press.

Hilliard, A.G. (1995) *Testing African-American students*. Chicago: Third World Press.

Jahn, J. (1961) *Muntu: The New African Culture*. New York: Grove Press.

Karenga, M. (1995) Afrocentricity and multicultural education: Concept challenge and contribution. In B.P. Bowser, T. Jones and G.A. Young (eds) *Toward the Multicultural University* (pp. 41–64). Westport, CT: Praeger Publishers.

Key, M., Kollman, L. and Smith, E. (1971) Features of child Black English. In W. Mackey and T. Anderson (eds) *Bilingualism in Early Childhood*. MA: Newbury House.

Kraft, C.H. and Kirk-Greene, A.H.M. (1979) *Hausa*. New York: David McKay Co.

Krapp, G.E. (1924) *The English of the Negro*. New York: American Mercury.

Labov, W. (1975) *The Study of Nonstandard English*. Washington, DC: National Council of Teachers of English and Center for Applied Linguistics.

Labov, W. (1985) Increasing divergence of Black and White vernaculars. Introduction to the research reports. (Unpublished manuscript).

Labov, W. (1995) Can reading failure be reversed? A linguistic approach to the question. In V.L. Gadsen and D.A. Wagner (eds) *Literacy Among African American Youth: Issues in Learning, Teaching, and Schooling* (pp. 39–68). Cresskill, NJ: Hampton Press, Inc.

Ladefoged, P. (1968) *A Phonetic Study of West African Languages*. Cambridge: University Press.

Lehman, W.P. (1972) *Descriptive Linguistics: An Introduction*. New York: Random House, Inc.

McWhorter, J.H. (1997) Wasting energy on an illusion. *Black Scholar* 27 (1) 9–14.

O'Grady, W., Dobrovolsky, M. and Arnoff, M. (1993) *Contemporary Linguistics. An Introduction*. New York: St. Martin's Press.

Palmer, L.R. (1978) *Descriptive and Comparative Linguistics: A Critical Introduction*. London: Faber & Faber.

Payen-Bellisle, R. (1894) *Sons et formes du creole dans les Antilles*. Baltimore: Murphy.

Pfaff, C. (1971) *Historical and Structural Aspects Of Sociolinguistic Variation: The Copula of Black English*. Inglewood, CA: Southwest Regional Laboratory.

Romaine, S. (1994) *Language and Society. An Introduction to Sociolinguistics*. New York; Oxford University Press Inc.

Rowlands, E.C. (1979) *Yoruba*. New York: David McKay Company, Inc.

Smith, A. (1972) In M.K. Asante (ed.) *Language Communication and Rhetoric in Black America* (pp. 29–36). New York: Harper and Row.

Smith, E.A. (1978) The retention of the phonological, phonemic, and morpho-phonemic features of Africa in Afro-American Ebonics. *Department of Linguistics Seminar Papers Series No. 43*. Fullerton, CA: California State University.

Smith, E.A. (1994) *The Historical Development of African American Language*. Los Angeles CA: Watts College Press.

Smith, E.A. (1995) Bilingualism and the African American child. In M.B. Joshua-Shearer, B.E. Pugh and B.A. Schaudt (eds) *Reading: The Blending of Theory and Practice* (pp. 83–95). Bakersfield, CA: California State University.

Smith, E.A. (1997) What is Black English? What is Ebonics? *Rethinking Schools* Fall.

Smitherman, G. (ed.) (1981) *Black English and the Education of Black Children and Youth*. Detroit, MI: Harlo Press.

Smitherman, G. (1994) *Black Talk*. Boston: Houghton Mifflin.

Turner, L.D. (1974) *Africanisms in the Gullah Dialect*. Ann Arbor, MI: The University of Michigan Press.

Vass, W.K. (1979) *The Bantu Speaking Heritage of the United States*. Los Angeles: Center for Afro-American Studies-UCLA.

Wardaugh, R. (1972) *Introduction to Linguistics*. New York: McGraw-Hill Book Company.

Webster's Third New International Dictionary (1971).

Welmers, W.E. (1973) *African Language Structures*. Berkeley, CA: University of California Press.

Whinnom, K. (1956) *The Origin of the European Based Creoles and Pidgins*. London: Orbis.

Williams, R.L. (1975) *Ebonics: the True Language of Black Folks*. St. Louis, MO: Institute of Black Studies.

Wolfram, W. (1972) Sociolinguistic premises and the nature of non-standard dialects. In A. Smith (ed.) *Language Communication and Rhetoric in Black America* (pp. 29–36). New York: Harper and Row.

Language Varieties in the School Curriculum: Where Do They Belong and How Will They Get There?

CAROLYN TEMPLE ADGER

The Ebonics debate has exposed a number of the myths that persist within the society, including K-12 education and teacher education, regarding varieties of English – particularly the myth of one true, invariant English. Interpretations of the Oakland School District's language policy have revealed the widespread perception that Ebonics, or African American Vernacular English (AAVE), reflects an inaccurate aim at Standard English. It may be possible to exploit the current focus on dialect to expose these myths and move the school curriculum toward conformity with the extensive body of sociolinguistic research about language variation. The understanding that varieties of a language differ from each other in patterned ways should be much more fully represented in the curriculum that is taught in schools than it is at present. This information is important for speakers of any dialect. Students need to understand that Standard English dialects are not inherently better than vernacular ones, although they may be socially preferred in some settings, and that all dialects serve important social functions. Had the public been better informed about patterned variability in language structure and use, the Ebonics debate might not have been so rancorous.

Others in this volume have explored important implications of scientific knowledge about vernacular dialects – in fact, all dialects – for schools. I have two additional points. The first is that accurate, detailed dialect information needs to be conveyed to students beginning in the primary years and extending to grade twelve. Meeting this goal requires development of curricular units and instructional materials. The second point is that the curriculum needs to incorporate accurate, detailed information about dialect appropriateness according to conversational setting. Popular notions about appropriateness in classrooms may be at odds with the ways that dialects actually function in schools.

These two points have implications for the reform of teacher education at a time when it is under intense scrutiny (National Commission on Teaching and America's Future, 1996; American Federation of Teachers, 2000). Updating the school language curriculum to more accurately reflect what is known about language variation will mean that teacher preparation will have to abandon the myth of a uniform Standard English and adopt a more complex view that is open to new understandings from research (Fillmore & Snow, 2002).

Dialect Awareness

We do not have adequate research concerning what children are taught in school about language variation, but it seems to be the case that language education favors prescription with little attention to linguistic description. The body of knowledge about dialects assembled by sociolinguists has had little impact on what students learn about language in the schools.

All children need to learn basic scientific information about how dialects work. The reasons are many, but one of the most important concerns the fact that we live in a multicultural world. Learning that languages vary geographically and socially in systematic ways is fundamental to combating the view that some people use a flawed English. But changing social attitudes takes time. Because negative attitudes toward vernacular dialects are not easily overcome, schools may want to provide instruction in a second dialect for speakers of vernacular dialects, including AAVE, as a way of enhancing students' access to educational and career opportunities. Robust understandings about contrasts in dialect structure and use are essential to this enterprise. Instruction must orient to adding the second dialect rather than replacing the first and using students' proficiency in the first dialect as the basis of second dialect development.

Educational policies are already in place to support dialect education. The *Standards for the English Language Arts* (NCTE/IRA, 1995) developed by the two leading professional organizations concerned with the school curriculum for language and literacy, the National Council of Teachers of English and the International Reading Association, assert that 'students [should] develop an understanding of and respect for diversity in language use, patterns, and dialects' (NCTE/IRA, 1995: 3). State departments of education have used the NCTE/IRA standards to develop standards and curriculum frameworks of their own, which in turn have become the basis for school district standards and curriculum development.

As difficult as it is to reach consensus on curriculum standards and the curricula derived from them, the existence of curriculum policy specifying what students should know and be able to do does not ensure that instruction will change. Teachers have an overwhelming array of responsibilities, which are constantly revised and added to. When the curriculum for dialect instruction changes radically, they cannot implement it without analyzing the relevant standards to determine what concepts and skills they entail, identifying instructional approaches and materials for students, and enhancing their own knowledge about dialects. Based on this analysis, units and lessons can be developed.

One avenue toward implementing the new research-based standards in classrooms is developing dialect awareness curricular units that help to make students more aware of some details of the dialects used in their locale and introduce them to the general sociolinguistic principles underlying dialect differences so that they can examine social attitudes toward dialects. Several models for such units have been developed.

Over the past decade, Walt Wolfram and his colleagues and students have been developing and pilot-testing dialect awareness units for upper elementary and middle-school students (e.g. Wolfram *et al.*, 1997). Students are introduced to social attitudes about dialects by viewing and discussing the video *American Tongues* (Alvarez & Kolker, 1987). They learn that dialects contrast on phonological, syntactic, and lexical features by listening to recordings of Appalachian storytellers and identifying the language levels to which certain features belong. Analyzing recorded data sets from different geographical regions, students derive the descriptive rules that account for phonological patterns, such as the absence of a vowel difference before nasal consonants (e.g. *pin* and *pen*) in Southern dialects or the deletion of the *r* sound following vowels and before consonants in some New England dialects. Students use their language intuitions to discover regularities in data sets from their own social dialects and those of others in their own community. In the process of observing and describing data from several dialects, they increase awareness of how dialects contrast.

The following exercise from a dialect curriculum exemplifies. It concerns habitual *be* in AAVE, a structure that has been mentioned often in the Ebonics conversation because it encodes a meaning that is not represented by a comparable lexical item in Standard English.

be in AAVE

Now, we're going to look at a form that's used in a dialect that is sometimes used by young African American speakers in large cities. The form *be* is used where other dialects use *am*, *is*, or *are*, except that it has a special meaning. People who use this dialect can tell where it may be used and where it may not be. . . In the sentences given here, choose one of the sentences in each pair where *be* fits better. Choose only one sentence for each pair. If you're not sure of the answer, simply make your best guess. Put a check next to the answer you think is right. *Do this work by yourself*.

1. ____ a. They usually be tired when they come home.
   ____ b. They be tired right now.
2. ____ a. When we play basketball, she be on my team.
   ____ b. The girl in the picture be my sister.
3. ____ a. James be coming to school right now.
   ____ b. James always be coming to school.
4. ____ a. Wanda don't usually be in school.
   ____ b. Wanda don't be in school today.
5. ____ a. My ankle be broken from the fall.
   ____ b. Sometimes my ears be itching.

(Wolfram *et al.*, 1999: 199)

Working through this data set, students describe the pattern that underlies it: Uninflected *be* indicates that the action occurs regularly. Sentences la, 2a, 3b, 4a, and 5b are grammatical in AAVE, but the others are not. Sentence 1b presents a present state, and sentence 2b concerns a constant state. Both contrast with the habitual state. This pattern can be difficult to identify. When these curricular materials were used in a fourth and fifth-grade class in Baltimore, MD, in which African American speakers of AAVE predominated (Wolfram *et al.*, 1992), the students had no difficulty with this task, but it often defeats speakers of other dialects, who do not have reliable intuitions about uninflected *be*.

After students have examined data on dialect pronunciation and grammar and formulated descriptive rules, they are assigned to collect data in the community. In one setting, students gathered data on lexical items, asking people in their community, 'How do you refer to your father's sister?' Most White students reported *aunt* ('ant') and most Black students reported *aunt* (rhyming with font). Students were fascinated to see the strong correlation between pronunciation of this common term and the ethnicity of the informant.

In addition to learning that dialects are rule-governed, students benefit from this approach to dialect study by experiencing the scientific method. They realize that it is used in the study of language just as it is in the study of other natural phenomena. Students might check a hypothesis developed for habitual *be* by collecting more data and then using it to predict where *be* could occur. They would be able to explain why the following sentence is not grammatical: 'After all, Ebonics be a complex issue' (Cosby, 1997).

Another curricular unit, by Kirk Hazen, emphasizes the ubiquity of variation. It includes an activity that leads students to realize that variation is typical of standard dialects as well as vernacular ones. This exercise has students indicate how the past tense marker -*ed* is pronounced in a list of verbs. Students learn that variation is constrained in this case by features of the final consonant in the root word. Another activity makes the point that languages change over time and that variability is a factor in the change process.

Dialect awareness units are quite appropriate in the English language arts curriculum because they address dialect standards, but teachers may also want to integrate a dialect study into multidisciplinary or thematic units. Thematic units often pair English language arts and social sciences. Attention to dialects can be included as the curriculum focuses on a geographical area of the USA or on population migration. Thematic units pairing English language arts and science can apply the scientific method to the study of language phenomena as well as the study of physical phenomena.

Dialect awareness units introduce basic ways of thinking about language on which subsequent study can build. Curricular attention to dialect awareness is relevant also to the necessity of fostering respect for group differences. In a culturally diverse society like ours, we must guide students to the understanding that respect is warranted by the fact that differences are differences and not defects. The claim that dialects are equal is not a matter of tolerating errors. Rodney King's poignant question, 'Why can't we all just get along?' is important for students to consider deeply. Part of the explanation for our society's difficulty with regard to differences is that we have been content to foster disrespect by perpetuating beliefs about culturally patterned ways that are unsupported by fact – in the present case, ways with words. A dialect awareness curriculum shows that the ways we are different from each other are not the result of failing to meet a single shared standard but the result of succeeding in meeting diverse standards. Difference is quite systematic, quite natural, and quite interesting.

These dialect awareness materials are not intended for large-scale implementation. Rather they serve as models for curriculum units that might be developed in other settings, incorporating descriptions of local dialects. The positive reaction of students who have studied dialects, in terms of increasing linguistic knowledge and questioning language prejudice, is promising.

Appropriateness

One of the tough nuts to crack in changing knowledge and attitudes for both teachers and students is the prevailing view of dialects and education, which holds that vernacular dialects are never appropriate in academic settings (Lucas & Borders, 1994). Used in this sense, *appropriateness* has a prescriptive force regarding how people ought to use language. This sort of appropriateness concerns ideals about language usage.

The term *appropriateness* is also used to refer to demonstrated social norms. This sort of appropriateness includes the actual expectations that people have for each other's language performance, as opposed to ideals. These norms are for the most part implicit. We have expectations about what it means to use language well and how people will use dialect features in different settings and interactive conditions.

A three-year qualitative study of dialect use in five elementary schools in Baltimore, MD, found that what happens in classrooms in that city did not conform to popular notions concerning where Standard English is appropriate, in what settings and what situations. I have casually observed this to be true in other schools in other cities. The Baltimore schools served students from poor and working class backgrounds. In three of them, all students and most teachers were African American. Students in the other two schools were both Black and White. Repeated observation suggested that almost all of the students were vernacular dialect speakers.

It has been loudly voiced in the Ebonics debate that vernacular dialects have no place in the classroom, that the dialect of teaching and learning is Standard English. But in the schools I studied, vernacular dialects were used quite regularly in academic discourse. In the classroom, students usually used vernacular dialect and teachers usually used standard dialect. But students shifted toward the standard end of the dialect continuum for more formal kinds of discourse, as would be expected (Labov, 1972; Wolfram, 1969). Formality derived from the nature of the instructional task and/or from the social role or footing (Goffman, 1981) that the speaker assumed. The situations in which students used Standard English features occurred especially in literacy events where students took part in literary analysis, as well as on those occasions in which teachers asked students to explain something to the class, such as how to complete a catalog order form. When this happened, students were speaking with authority on the topic at hand in the way that teachers do much of the time. Any situation in which students were asked to speak authoritatively to other class members made shifting toward Standard English appropriate in the classrooms studied.

This analysis relies on Erving Goffman's (1981) notion of footing and the sociolinguistic notion of register. Goffman points out that one way in which speakers convey meaning is by indicating an alignment toward their audience as they speak. Shifting alignment within a discourse activity may be conveyed by shifting register – the 'conventionalized lexical, syntactic and prosodic choices deemed appropriate for the setting and audience' (Tannen & Wallat, 1993: 63). In the classrooms, students used the resources of standard and vernacular dialects to indicate their stance toward each other and toward their topics. Normally, they used vernacular features during lesson discourse led by the teacher in which students spoke as learners, not experts on the topic at hand. But occasionally teachers asked them to speak with some expertise or unique understanding. As they assumed an authoritative footing, students used more standard features and avoided vernacular features. Thus in a discussion of the plot structure of Rumpelstiltskin, Kevin responded to the teacher's question about the story's problem by saying, 'The problem... the *prob*lem is... that the king... wants gold.' He produced the copula *is* and the third person agreement marker /s/ on the verb *want*, features that may be deleted in AAVE (the segment that includes this example is discussed in more detail in Adger, 1998, and in Adger & Wolfram, 1999.) There are two explanations for the fact that Kevin, a proficient speaker of AAVE, avoided deletion here. First, in this activity students were dictating sentences to be written by the teacher, and Standard English is more clearly associated with writing than with oral language. But the association with writing was not the only factor. Elsewhere students exhibited a similar shift toward Standard English when they were not dictating. In this instance, Kevin was speaking with authority as he answered the question about the story's problem.

Subsequent talk showed that the teacher's request was for Kevin to express his particular interpretation of the text. Other students had different ideas about the story's central problem, and they, too, used Standard English features in explaining them.

In the Baltimore classrooms, teachers and students alike demonstrated through their instructional discourse that students were expected to use vernacular features except when teachers invited them to speak with the authority of expert knowledge. When they failed to use Standard English under these conditions, the teacher did correct the students' grammatical choices.

Implications of Dialect Shifting in Classroom Discourse

Such details of language use in classrooms are probably not within the awareness of teachers and students. But if teachers assert that Standard English is always appropriate for school talk, students have reason to doubt them. It simply isn't so. Perpetuating a myth about dialect distribution is one way of inviting students to opt out of classroom participation (Piestrup, 1973; Smitherman, 1977).

Investigating how dialects actually function at school can be part of dialect education for educators, both teachers and teacher educators. It can contribute to conversations about the functions of dialects, which can go far toward explaining the perseverance of vernacular dialects in the face of public scorn. Teachers can study the distribution of vernacular and standard dialects within their own classrooms by taping classroom interaction and listening closely. They will discover the range of dialectal choices that students make and note the triggers for shifting along the dialect continuum. This exercise will allow accurate statements about dialect appropriateness for promoting Standard English development, and it will give teachers insight into their students' skill in using language strategically.

There is another reason for teachers to examine dialect distribution in their own classrooms. In interviews from the Baltimore study, teachers reiterated the traditional claim that students should use Standard English. Investigating the actual sociolinguistic norms followed by the teachers and their students gave the very different and more complex picture summarized here. Teachers of bidialectal students need to ask whether the discourse conditions in their classrooms provide sufficient opportunity for students to shift toward Standard English, given the implicit classroom community norms for dialect choice. Telling students to speak Standard English consistently and 'correcting' vernacular features leads to more, not less, use of vernacular items (Piestrup, 1973). Students cannot be expected to increase their production of Standard English unless the sociolinguistic conditions for its use are operating. The social penalties for flouting the local norms for elite language use are simply too onerous (Fordham, 1998). But when the conditions favoring Standard English do operate, students produce standard features without being told to do so, as this study showed. Likewise, students do not need to be told to learn Standard English because they will need it for job mobility or advanced education in the future. Standard English is a present need for them when the conditions are right.

In many classrooms, teacher-centered direct instruction continues to predominate, and students have relatively few opportunities to speak with authority, despite research on the importance of active learning (Bransford *et al.*, 2000). It has been estimated that even when teachers involve their students in discussion, students have two-thirds of the turns at talk. The remaining one-third is shared by all of the 30 or so students in the classroom and controlled, more or less, by the teacher (Cazden, 2001). But the opportunities for talk within this one-third portion are probably not distributed evenly across the population of students. Who gets to talk are the students who are adept at attracting teacher nomination or jumping into the lesson talk and helping to advance it. With time, participation opportunities are no longer so equally distributed because the classroom community comes to realize whose talk has highest status. Some students' rights to speak with authority are clearer than those of others. (Kevin, who answered the teacher's question about the problem in *Rumpelstiltskin*, often self-nominated and was often called on to speak with authority.)

In advocating that teachers create opportunities for students to speak with authority so that Standard English will be called for, I am not suggesting that the vernacular dialect is not also valuable. Geneva Smitherman (this volume) highlighted the importance of preserving the vernacular dialect and promoting students' developing expertise in it. AAVE plays an important role in communication and in demonstrating social identity and solidarity across African American communities, and most African American students need to have some level of proficiency in it (Rickford & Rickford, 2000). This includes knowing implicitly when to shift toward which direction of the dialect continuum and having the sociolinguistic resources for doing so.

The evidence of dialect shifting discussed here came from a classroom in which all of the students and the teacher were African American. In many classrooms, teachers do not share ethnicity and/or dialect with their students. Teachers who are not members of the speech community of their students need to see that students use different dialects expertly in the classroom. During preservice education and throughout their careers, teachers can profit from experiences in their students' communities that enhance their awareness of social dialects. Teachers need to know what they can do to enhance students' proficiency in the dialects that they need across settings.

Implications for Teacher Preparation

In order to improve dialect education for students, teachers need considerable knowledge in this domain. Recently developed standards for teachers and for teacher preparation make clear that teachers must have knowledge about language variation (Gollnick, 2002; National Council for Accreditation of Teacher Education and Association for Childhood Education International, 2000; National Council of Teachers of English, 1996).

Improving teachers' ability to provide accurate dialect education is likely to call for changing attitudes as well. As a result of our socialization, our education, and language attitudes that permeate the society, adults' attitudes toward vernacular dialects may be quite negative. Even when they engage in dialect awareness activities, many teachers initially resist the notion that structural regularity amounts to dialect equality. As their knowledge builds, they may be unsure about how to reassess the traditional prescriptive view of dialects in light of the scientific view and how to plan Standard English instruction for their students. If they show students contrasts between standard and vernacular dialects, how should they handle evaluative comments from students and parents? How can they balance students' intuitions about language norms with their language prejudices?

Significant changes in teacher preparation appear to be warranted to enable teachers to teach students about English in a diverse world. But because teacher education courses and to a great extent course content are mandated by state departments of education, modifying teacher preparation is very difficult. And there are demands for new topics and new courses from many directions (Richardson, 2002). In-service training is another important venue for teacher development. Dialect education for teachers linked to implementing dialect curricula for students may be possible for school districts, especially in partnership with universities.

Approaches and materials making dialect education practical have been developed in the past few years. Innovative, sound approaches being used now in some teacher-preparation institutions could be disseminated (e.g. Wheeler & Swords, in press). What is needed is a means of identifying these practices, testing their effectiveness, and making them available for others to replicate or emulate. Some linguists have contributed to designing and providing in-service professional development that refines the knowledge, skills, and attitudes regarding dialects that teachers need in order to support accurate linguistic understanding among their students. Others who would like to do so can team with colleagues who are well versed in the practices and traditions of schools and teacher education. Associations such as the Linguistic Society of America might contribute by marshalling volunteers to work with educators on developing locally relevant dialect awareness curricula and collecting course syllabi for teacher education. Texts appropriate for teachers have appeared in the last few years (e.g. Wolfram _et al_., 1999). Nontechnical books for general audiences can be useful as well (e.g. Baugh, 2000; McWhorter, 1998; Rickford & Rickford, 2000). The American Speech-Language-Hearing Association will soon release a CD for training speech/language pathologists on the structure of AAVE to enhance their ability to assess language development. This resource will be useful to educators as well.

Given the prevailing view of language variation, however, sustaining changes in teacher education and in K-12 education so that dialects are understood and respected will take more than appropriate resources and programs. It will take more than a well intended nod to differences in teacher education and professional development. It will take more than two weeks or even a semester in a class on multiculturalism. It will take serious, sustained attention to sociolinguistic education at the very least. We have an opportunity now in the context of the interest in Ebonics that continues in education and in the public consciousness. We need to move as soon as we can and with as much force as we can, as fast as we can to change dialect education in our schools.

References

Adger, C.T. (1998) Register shifting with dialect resources in instructional discourse. In S. Hoyle and C.T. Adger (eds) _Kids Talk: Strategic Language Use in Later Childhood_. New York: Oxford.

Adger, C.T. and Wolfram, W. (1999) Demythologizing the home/school dichotomy: Sociolinguistic reality and instructional practice. In P. Griffin, J. Peyton, W. Wolfram and R.W. Fasold (eds) _Language in Action: New Studies of Language in Society_. New York: Hampton.

Adger, C., Wolfram, W., Detwyler, J. and Harry, B. (1993) Confronting dialect minority issues in special education: Reactive and proactive perspectives. In

Proceedings of the Third National Research Symposium on Limited English Proficient Student Issues. Focus on Middle and High School Issues (pp. 737–762). Washington, DC: US Department of Education, Office of Bilingual Education and Minority Languages Affairs.

Alvarez, L. and Kolker, A. (producers) (1987) *American Tongues* [Video]. New York: Center for New American Media.

American Federation of Teachers (2000) *Building a Profession: Strengthening Teacher Preparation and Induction*. Washington, DC: American Federation of Teachers.

Baugh, J. (2000) *Beyond Ebonics: Linguistic Pride and Racial Prejudice*. New York: Oxford.

Bransford, J.D., Brown, A.L. and Cocking, R. (eds) (2000) *How People Learn: Brain, Mind, Experience, and School*. Washington: National Academy Press.

Cazden, C. (1988) *Classroom Discourse*. Portsmouth, NH: Heinemann.

Cosby, B. (1997) Elements of igno-Ebonics style. *Wall Street Journal* January 10.

Fillmore, L.W. and Snow, C.E. (2002) What teachers need to know about language. In C.T. Adger, C.E. Snow, and D. Christian (eds) *What Teachers Need to Know about Language* (pp. 7–54). Washington, DC, and McHenry, IL: Center for Applied Linguistics and Delta Systems.

Fordham, S. (1998) Speaking standard English from nine to three: Language as guerrilla warfare at Capital High. In S. Hoyle and C.T. Adger (eds) *Kids Talk: Strategic Language Use in Later Childhood* (pp. 205–216). New York: Oxford.

Goffman, E. (1981) *Footing: Forms of Talk*. Philadelphia: University of Pennsylvania Press.

Gollnick, D.M. (2002) Incorporating linguistic knowledge in standards for teacher performance. In C.T. Adger, C.E. Snow and D. Christian (eds) *What Teachers Need to Know about Language* (pp. 103–112). Washington, DC, and McHenry, IL: Center for Applied Linguistics and Delta Systems.

Hazen, K. (2001) Teaching about dialects. *ERIC Digest* (October). On WWW at www.cal.org/ericcll/digest/0104dialects.html.

Labov, W. (1972) *Language in the Inner City: Studies in the Black English Vernacular*. Philadelphia: University of Pennsylvania Press.

Lucas, C. and Borders, D. (1994) *Language Diversity and Classroom Discourse*. Norwood, NJ: Ablex.

McWhorter, R. (1998) *The Word on the Street: Debunking the Myth of Pure Standard English*. New York: Plenum.

National Commission on Teaching and America's Future (1996) *What Matters Most: Teaching for America's Future*. New York: National Commission on Teaching and America's Future.

National Council for Accreditation of Teacher Education and Association for Childhood Education Internation (2000) *Program Standards for Elementary Teacher Preparation*. On WWW at http://www.udel.edu/bateman/acei/nca-teindex.htm.

National Council of Teachers of English (1996) *Guidelines for the Preparation of Teachers of English Language Arts*. Urbana, IL: National Council of Teachers of English.

National Council of Teachers of English and the International Reading Association (1996) *Standards for the English Language Arts*. Newark, DE: Authors.

Piestrup, A.M. (1973) *Black dialect interference and accommodations of reading instruction in first grade* (Monograph 4). Berkeley, CA: California University, Berkeley, Language and Behavior Research Lab. (ED 119 113).

Richardson, V. (2002) Teacher knowledge about language. In C.T. Adger, C.E. Snow and D. Christian (eds) *What Teachers Need to Know About Language* (pp. 85–102). Washington, DC, and McHenry, IL: Center for Applied Linguistics and Delta Systems.

Rickford, J. and Rickford, R. (2000) *Spoken Soul: The Story of Black English*. New York: Wiley.

Smitherman, G. (1977) *Talkin and Testifyin: The Language of Black America*. Detroit: Wayne State University Press.

Tannen, D. and Wallat, C. (1993) Interactive frames and knowledge schemas in interaction. In D. Tannen (ed.) *Framing in Discourse*. New York: Oxford.

Wheeler, R. and Swords, R. (in press) Codeswitching: Tools of language and culture transform the dialectally diverse classroom. *Language Arts*.

Wolfram, W. (1969) *A Linguistic Description of Detroit Negro Speech*. Washington, DC: Center for Applied Linguistics.

Wolfram, W., Adger, C. and Christian, D. (1999) *Dialects in Schools and Communities*. Mahwah, NJ: Erlbaum.

Wolfram, W., Adger, C. and Detwyler, D. (1992) *All About Dialects*. Washington, DC: Center for Applied Linguistics.

Wolfram, W., Schilling-Estes, N. and Hazen, K. (1997) *Dialects and the Ocracoke Brogue: An 8th Grade Curriculum*. Raleigh, NC: North Carolina Language and Life Project.

Part 2
Background To The
Ebonics Debate

Introduction

Part 2 of this collection brings together additional background materials and documents on the Ebonics debate. It is intended to help the reader contextualize the preceding discussion and to provide additional perspectives on the topic. Included first is the original resolution by the Oakland Unified School District (OUSD). It was this resolution that initiated the most recent in a series of Ebonics controversies spanning over the last three and a half decades. The debate over Ebonics has involved students, parents, educators, school districts, linguists, politicians, lawyers, judges, and – of course – the ever-present media. Nevertheless, it is important to recognize that the struggle to affirm the language of African Americans did not just begin recently in Oakland. As was noted, Carter G. Woodson was denouncing the denigration of African American language in education in the early 1930s. Following the initial Oakland resolution is the OUSD's subsequent clarification that attempted to explain and clarify some of the more contentious aspects of the initial resolution.

The section on 'Examples of Legislative Reaction' provides cases of the restrictive and punitive legislation that was rashly drafted in response to the media spectacle that followed the initial OUSD resolution. Particularly telling was the attempt to legislate the 'illegitimacy' of Ebonics as a 'language' and the punitive attempt to remove funds from districts that would attempt to recognize it as a legitimate language of communication. Equally instructive was the co-opting of egalitarian rhetoric as a cover for restrictive language polices. S.B. 205, for example, was dubbed the *'Equality in English Instruction Act'* (italics added).

Next follows excerpts from the 1979 legal case (*Martin Luther King Junior Elementary School Children* et al. *v. Ann Arbor School District Board,* 473 E Supp. 1371) in Ann Arbor, Michigan that has been discussed by several of our authors. As they have noted, the case was important because it relied upon the testimony of linguists to establish the legitimacy of African American language. Unfortunately, the decision failed to acknowledge the relationship between language discrimination, or what Tove Skutnabb-Kangas and Robert Phillipson have called 'linguicism,' and racism (see Phillipson, 1989; Phillipson *et al.*, 1994).

Moreover, because the case was decided in a federal district court and was not appealed, it did not have the impact of a Supreme Court decision.

In 'Linguists' Reactions,' additional perspectives of several well known authorities are included. Following the initial OUSD resolution, Professor Charles Fillmore wrote a thoughtful critique in an effort to contrast putative assumptions from scholarly understanding. Professor Walt Wolfram, a longtime veteran of the controversy, provides a medley of key issues, including the official perspective of the Linguistic Society of America (LSA). Professor Rickford, courtesy of the Center for Applied Linguistics (CAL), provides a concise historical snapshot on the related controversy regarding whether or not 'dialect readers' should be used as a bridge to literacy for African American students. Then, the expert-advocate voice of Professor William Labov informs Congress on the history of research on the legitimacy of African American Vernacular English/Ebonics as a legitimate variety of language.

In the section 'Organizational Responses,' the position of Teachers of English to Speakers of Other Languages (TESOL) underscores the major points made by Dr Adger. The resolution of the American Association for Applied Linguistics lends the authority of the major applied professional organization as does the CAL Media Statement. (Again, note the position of the LSA in Professor Wolfram's section.) The California Association for Bilingual Education's 'Position Statement: Ebonics' points to the need to make connections between issues of bilingualism and bidialectism.

The final section in this volume, 'Recommended Readings on Ebonics,' provides a comprehensive bibliography of the major scholarly work that has been published in this field over the last 40 years. This section also includes a list of news titles that provides a glimpse into perceptions of Ebonics in the mass print media.

References

Phillipson, R. (1989) Linguicism: Structures and ideologies in linguistic imperialism. In T. Skutnabb-Kangas and J. Cummins (eds) *Minority Education: From Shame to Struggle* (pp. 339–358). Clevedon, UK: Multilingual Matters.

Phillipson, R.M., Rannut, T. and Skutnabb-Kangas, T. (1994) Introduction. In T. Skutnabb-Kangas and R. Phillipson (eds) *Linguistic Human Rights: Overcoming Linguistic Discrimination* (pp. 1–22). Berlin: Mouton de Gruyter.

Oakland Unified School District's Resolution

ORIGINAL OAKLAND UNIFIED SCHOOL DISTRICT RESOLUTION ON EBONICS

December, 1996

RESOLUTION OF THE BOARD OF EDUCATION ADOPTING THE REPORT AND RECOMMENDATIONS OF THE AFRICAN-AMERICAN TASK FORCE; A POLICY STATEMENT AND DIRECTING THE SUPERINTENDENT OF SCHOOLS TO DEVISE A PROGRAM TO IMPROVE THE ENGLISH LANGUAGE ACQUISITION AND APPLICATION SKILLS OF AFRICAN-AMERICAN STUDENTS. No. 9597-0063

WHEREAS, numerous validated scholarly studies demonstrate that African American students as part of their culture and history as African people possess and utilize a language described in various scholarly approaches as "Ebonics" (literally Black sounds) or Pan African Communication Behaviors or African Language Systems; and

WHEREAS, these studies have also demonstrated that African Language Systems are genetically-based and not a dialect of English; and

WHEREAS, these studies demonstrate that such West and Niger-Congo African languages have been officially recognized and addressed in the mainstream public educational community as worth of study, understanding or application of its principles, laws and structures for the benefit of African American students both in terms of positive appreciation of the language and these students' acquisition and mastery of English language skills; and

WHEREAS, such recognition by scholars has given rise over the past 15 years to legislation passed by the State of California recognizing the unique language stature of descendants of slaves, with such legislation being prejudicially and unconstitutionally vetoed repeatedly by various California state governors; and

115

WHEREAS, judicial cases in states other than California have recognized the unique language stature of African American pupils, and such recognition by courts has resulted in court-mandated educational programs which have substantially benefited African American children in the interest of vindicating their equal protection of the law rights under the 14th Amendment to the United States Constitution; and

WHEREAS, the Federal Bilingual Education Act (20 USC 1402 et seq.) mandates that local educational agencies "build their capacities to establish, implement and sustain programs of instruction for children and youth of limited English proficiency," and

WHEREAS, the interests of the Oakland Unified School District in providing equal opportunities for all of its students dictate limited English proficient educational programs recognizing the English language acquisition and improvement skills of African American students are as fundamental as is application of bilingual education principles for others whose primary languages are other than English; and

WHEREAS, the standardized tests and grade scores of African American students in reading and language art skills measuring their application of English skills are substantially below state and national norms and that such deficiencies will be remedied by application of a program featuring African Language Systems principles in instructing African American children both in their primary language and in English, and

WHEREAS, standardized tests and grade scores will be remedied by application of a program with teachers and aides who are certified in the methodology of featuring African Language Systems principles in instructing African American children both in their primary language and in English. The certified teachers of these students will be provided incentives including, but not limited to salary differentials,

NOW, THEREFORE, BE IT RESOLVED that the Board of Education officially recognizes the existence and the cultural and historic bases of West and Niger-Congo African Language Systems, and each language as the predominantly primary language of African American students; and

BE IT FURTHER RESOLVED that the Board of Education hereby adopts the report recommendations and attached Policy Statement of the District's African American Task Force on language stature of African American speech; and

BE IT FURTHER RESOLVED that the Superintendent in conjunction with her staff shall immediately devise and implement the best possible academic program for imparting instruction to African American students in their primary language for the combined purposes of maintaining the legitimacy and richness of such language whether it is known as "Ebonics," "African Language Systems," "Pan African Communication Behaviors" or other description, and to facilitate their acquisition and mastery of English language skills; and

BE IT FURTHER RESOLVED that the Board of Education hereby commits to earmark District general and special funding as is reasonably necessary and appropriate to enable the Superintendent and her staff to accomplish the foregoing; and

BE IT FURTHER RESOLVED that the Superintendent and her staff shall utilize the input of the entire Oakland educational community as well as state and federal scholarly and educational input in devising such a program; and

BE IT FURTHER RESOLVED, that periodic reports on the progress of the creation and implementation of such an educational program shall be made to Board of Education at least once per month commencing at the Board meeting of December 18, 1996.

POLICY STATEMENT

There is persuasive empirical evidence that, predicated on analysis of the phonology, morphology and syntax that currently exists as systematic, rule governed and predictable patterns exist in the grammar of African-American speech. The validated and persuasive linguistic evidence is that African-Americans

(1)   have retained a West and Niger-Congo African linguistic structure in the substratum of their speech and
(2)   by this criteria are not native speakers of black dialect or any other dialect of English.

Moreover, there is persuasive empirical evidence that, owing to their history as United States slave descendants of West and Niger-Congo African origin, to the extent that African-Americans have been born into, reared in, and continue to live in linguistic environments that are different from the Euro-American English speaking population, African-American people and their children, are from home environments in which a language other than English language is dominant within the meaning of "environment where a Language other than English is dominant" as defined in Public Law 113-382 (20 U.S.C. 7402, et seq.).

The policy of the Oakland Unified School District (OUSD) is that all pupils are equal and are to be treated equally. Hence, all pupils who have difficulty speaking, reading, writing or understanding the English language and whose difficulties may deny to them the opportunity to learn successfully in classrooms where the language of instruction is English or to participate fully in classrooms where the language of instruction is English or to participate fully in our society are to be treated equally regardless of their race or national origin.

As in the case of Asian-American, Latino-American, Native American and all other pupils in this District who come from backgrounds or environments where a language other than English is dominant, African-American pupils shall not, because of their race, be subtly dehumanized, stigmatized, discriminated against or denied. Asian-American, Latino-American, Native American and all other language different children are provided general funds for bilingual education, English as Second Language (ESL) and State and Federal (Title VII) bilingual education programs to address their limited and non-English proficient (LEP/NEP) needs. African-American pupils are equally entitled to be tested and, where appropriate, shall be provided general funds and State and

Federal (Title VII) bilingual education and ESL programs to specifically address their LEP/NEP needs.

All classroom teachers and aides who are bilingual in Nigritian Ebonics (African-American Language) and English shall be given the same salary differentials and merit increases that are provided to teachers of the non-African American LEP pupils in the OUSD.

With a view toward assuring that parents of African-American pupils are given the knowledge base necessary to make informed choices, it shall be the policy of the Oakland Unified School District that all parents of LEP (Limited English Proficient) pupils are to be provided the opportunity to partake of any and all language and culture specific teacher education and training classes designed to address their child's LEP needs.

On all home language surveys given to parents of pupils requesting home language identification or designations, a description of the District's programmatic consequences of their choices will be contained.

Nothing in this Policy shall preclude or prevent African-American parents who view their child's limited English proficiency as being nonstandard English, as opposed to being West and Niger-Congo African Language based, from exercising their right to choose and to have their child's speech disorders and English Language deficits addressed by special education and/or other District programs.

CLARIFICATION

OAKLAND UNIFIED SCHOOL DISTRICT (OUSD) SYNOPSIS OF THE ADOPTED POLICY ON STANDARD AMERICAN ENGLISH LANGUAGE DEVELOPMENT

On December 18, 1996 the Oakland Unified School District Board of Education approved a policy affirming Standard American English language development for all students. This policy states that effective instructional strategies must be utilized in order to ensure that every child has the opportunity to achieve English language proficiency. Language development for African American students, who comprise 53% of the students in the Oakland schools, will be enhanced with the recognition and understanding of the language structures unique to African American students. This language has been studied for several decades and is variously referred to as Ebonics (literally "Black sounds"), or "Pan-African Communication Behaviors," or "African Language Systems."

This policy is based on the work of a broad-based Task Force, convened six months ago to review the district-wide achievement data (see Appendix 1) and to make recommendations regarding effective practices that would enhance the opportunity for all students to successfully achieve the standards of the core curriculum (see Appendix 2). The data show low levels of student performance, disproportionately high representation in special education, and under-representation in Advanced Placement courses and in the Gifted and Talented Education Program. The recommendations (see Appendix 3), based on academic research, focus on the unique language stature of African American pupils, the direct connection of English language proficiency to student achievement, and the education of parents and the community to support academic achievement (see bibliography in Appendix 4).

One of the programs recommended is the Standard English Proficiency Program (S.E.P.), a State of California model program, which promotes English-language development for African American students. The S.E.P. training enables teachers and administrators to respect and acknowledge the history, culture, and language that the African American student brings to school. Recently a "Superliteracy" component was added to ensure the development of high levels of reading, writing, and speaking skills. The policy further requires strengthening pre-school education and parent and community participation in the educational processes of the District.

The recommendations of the Task Force establish English language proficiency as the foundation for competency in all academic areas. Passage of this policy is a clear demonstration that the Oakland Unified School District is committed to take significant actions to turn around the educational attainment of its African-American students.

(CLARIFICATION)

LEGISLATIVE INTENT
OAKLAND'S STANDARD: ENGLISH!

The Board of Education adopted a policy on teaching English, not Ebonics. Unfortunately, because of misconceptions in the resulting press stories, the actions of the Board of Education have been publicly misunderstood.

Misconceptions include:

- Oakland School District has decided to teach Ebonics in place of English.
- The District is trying to classify Ebonics (i.e. "Black English,") speaking students as bilingual.
- OUSD is only attempting to pilfer federal and state funds.
- OUSD is trying to create a system of perverse incentives that reward failure and lower standards.
- Oakland is condoning the use of slang.
- Oakland has gone too far.
- Ebonics further segregates an already racially divided school district.
- There is no statistical evidence to support this approach or that this approach will improve student achievement.

Nothing could be further from the truth.

- The Oakland Unified School District is not replacing the teaching of Standard American English with any other language. The District is not teaching Ebonics. The District emphasizes teaching Standard American English and has set a high standard of excellence for all its students.
- Oakland Unified School District is providing its teachers and parents with the tools to address the diverse languages the children bring into the classroom.
- The District's objective is to build on the language skills that African American students bring to the classroom without devaluing students and their diversity. We have directly connected English language proficiency to student achievement. *The term "genetically based" is synonymous with genesis.* In the clause, "African

Language Systems are genetically based and not a dialect of English," the term "genetically based" is used according to the standard dictionary definition of "has origins in." It is not used to refer to human biology (emphasis added).

(CLARIFICATION)

APPENDIX 1: OAKLAND UNIFIED SCHOOL DISTRICT FINDINGS

- 53% of the total Oakland Unified School District's enrollment of 51,706 is African American.
- 71% of the students enrolled in Special Education were African American.
- 37% of the students enrolled in GATE classes were African American.
- 64% of students retained were African American.
- 67% of students classified as truant were African American.
- 71% of African American males attend school on a regular basis.
- 19% of the 12th grade African American students did not graduate.
- 80% of all suspended students were African American.
- 1.80 average GPA of African American students represents the lowest GPA in the district.

(CLARIFICATION)

APPENDIX 2:
OUSD CORE CURRICULUM STANDARDS AT
BENCHMARK GRADE LEVELS

GRADE 1:

All students will read and perform mathematics at grade level.

GRADE 3:

All students will read at grade level, have mastery of mathematical operations, and compose written works on a computer.

GRADE 5:

All students will meet or exceed the fifth grade standards for the core curriculum in language Arts, Mathematics, Science, and Social Science.

GRADE 8:

All students will be able to read and engage with complex and diverse literature, conduct a research project and write a scholarly paper on that research, perform mathematics at a level required to enroll in Algebra, organize and participate in community service and social events, and utilize technology as a tool for learning and work.

GRADE 10:

All students will successfully complete college required coursework in English, Math, and Science, and will enroll in a career academy or program.

GRADE 12:

All students will successfully complete courses required for entrance into a college or university, meet the requirements for an entry level career position, and develop and defend a senior project.

(CLARIFICATION)

APPENDIX 3:
OVERVIEW OF OUSD RECOMMENDATIONS

The recommendations, based on identified conditions and outcomes, are aligned with the Content Standards adopted by OUSD, pre-kindergarten-12th grades, 1996–1997.

It is the consensus of the African American Task Force that the African American students' language needs have not been fully addressed.

This report addresses the language needs of African American students as one of the nine major areas of recommendations to be implemented by OUSD.

1. African American students shall develop English language proficiency as the foundation for their achievements in all core competency areas.
2. All existing programs shall be implemented fully to enhance the achievements of African American students.
3. The Task Force on the Education of African American Students shall be retained in order to assist OUSD in developing work plans and implementation strategies.
4. Financial commitments shall be made to implement the Task Force on the Education of African American Students recommendations during the current fiscal year.
5. The district's identification and assessment criteria for GATE and Special Education Programs shall be reviewed.
6. The community shall be mobilized to partner with OUSD to achieve recommended outcomes.
7. OUSD shall develop a policy which requires all categorical and general program funding to be used to ensure access to and mastery of the core curriculum.
8. All resources of the district shall be applied and used to ensure that these recommendations be implemented.
9. OUSD shall develop recruitment procedures that facilitate the hiring of administrators, teachers, counselors and support staff that reflect the culture of African American students composition of the student population.

"Black children are the proxy for what ails American education in general. And so, as we fashion solutions which help Black children, we fashion solutions which help all children."

The Honorable Augustus E. Hawkins

(CLARIFICATION) AMENDED RESOLUTION

OF THE BOARD OF EDUCATION ADOPTING THE REPORT AND RECOMMENDATIONS OF THE AFRICAN-AMERICAN TASK FORCE; A POLICY STATEMENT AND DIRECTING THE SUPERINTENDENT OF SCHOOLS TO DEVISE A PROGRAM TO IMPROVE THE ENGLISH LANGUAGE ACQUISITION AND APPLICATION SKILLS OF AFRICAN-AMERICAN STUDENTS No. 9697-0063

WHEREAS, numerous validated scholarly studies demonstrate that African-American students as a part of their culture and history as African people possess and utilize a language described in various scholarly approaches as "Ebonics" (literally "Black sounds") or "Pan African Communication Behaviors" or "African Language Systems"; and

WHEREAS, these studies have also demonstrated that African Language Systems have origins in West and Niger-Congo languages and are not merely dialects of English; and

WHEREAS, these studies demonstrate that such West and Niger-Congo African languages have been recognized and addressed in the educational community as worthy of study, understanding and application of their principles, laws and structures for the benefit of African-American students both in terms of positive appreciation of the language and these students' acquisition and mastery of English language skills; and

WHEREAS, such recognition by scholars has given rise over the past fifteen years to legislation passed by the State of California recognizing the unique language stature of descendants of slaves, with such legislation being vetoed repeatedly by various California state governors; and

WHEREAS, judicial cases in states other than California have recognized the unique language stature of African American pupils, and such recognition by courts has resulted in court-mandated educational programs which have substantially benefited African-American children in the interest of vindicating their equal protection of the law rights under the Fourteenth Amendment to the United States Constitution; and

WHEREAS, the Federal Bilingual Education Act (20 U.S.C. 1402 et seq.) mandates that local educational agencies "build their capacities to establish, implement and sustain programs of instruction for children and youth of limited English proficiency"; and

WHEREAS, the interest of the Oakland Unified School District in providing equal opportunities for all of its students dictate limited English proficient educational programs recognizing the English language acquisition and improvement skills of African American students are as fundamental as is application of bilingual or second language learner principles for others whose primary languages are other than English. Primary languages are the language patterns children bring to school; and

WHEREAS, the standardized tests and grade scores of African-American students in reading and language arts skills measuring their application of English skills are substantially below state and national norms and that such deficiencies shall be remedied by application of a program featuring African Language Systems principles to move students from the language patterns they bring to school to English proficiency; and

WHEREAS, standardized tests and grade scores will be remedied by application of a program that teachers and instructional assistants, who are certified in the methodology of African Language Systems principles used to transition students from the language patterns they bring to school to English. The certified teachers of these students will be provided incentives including, but not limited to, salary differentials;

NOW, THEREFORE, BE IT RESOLVED that the Board of Education officially recognizes the existence, and the cultural and historic bases of West and Niger-Congo African Language Systems, and these are the language patterns that many African-American students bring to school; and

BE IT FURTHER RESOLVED that the Board of Education hereby adopts the report, recommendations and attached Policy Statement of the District's African-American Task Force on the language stature of African-American speech; and

BE IT FURTHER RESOLVED that the Superintendent in conjunction with her staff shall immediately devise and implement the best possible academic program for the combined purposes of facilitating the acquisition and mastery of English language skills, while respecting and embracing the legitimacy and richness of the language patterns whether they are known as "Ebonics," "African Language Systems," "Pan African Communication Behaviors," or other description; and

BE IT FURTHER RESOLVED that the Board of Education hereby commits to earmark District general and special funding as is reasonably necessary and appropriate to enable the Superintendent and her staff to accomplish the foregoing; and

BE IT FURTHER RESOLVED that the Superintendent and her staff shall utilize the input of the entire Oakland educational community as well as state and federal scholarly and educational input in devising such a program; and

BE IT FURTHER RESOLVED that periodic reports on the progress of the creation and implementation of such an educational program shall be made to the Board of Education at least once per month commencing at the Board meeting of December 18, 1996.

Passed by the following vote:

AYES: Hodge, Cook, Rice, Harrison, Gallo, Vice President Spencer, President Quan
NOES: None
ABSTAINING: None
ABSENT: None

I hereby certify that the foregoing is a full, true and correct copy of an amended resolution passed at a Special Meeting of the Board of Education of the Oakland Unified School District held January 15, 1997.

s/ Edgar Rakestraw Jr.

Deputy Secretary of the Board of Education

(CLARIFICATION)

APPENDIX 4:
BIBLIOGRAPHY

Alleyne, M.C. (1971) Linguistic continuity of Africa in the Caribbean. In H.J. Richards (ed.) *Topics in Afro-American Studies* (pp. 119–134). New York: Black Academy Press.

Chomsky, N. (1972) *Language and Mind*. New York: Harcourt Brace, Janovich.

California Language Arts Framework (1987) Sacramento, CA: California Department of Education.

De Franz, A. (1994) Coming to cultural and linguistic awakening: An African and African American educational vision. In J. Frederickson (ed.) *Reclaiming our Voices: Bilingual Education Critical Pedagogy and Praxis*. Ontario, CA: California Association for Bilingual Education.

Delpit, L. (1988) The silenced dialogue: Power and pedagogy in educating other people's children. *Harvard Education Review* 58 (3).

Dillard, J.L. (1973) *Black English: Its History and Usage in the United States*. New York: Vintage Books.

Fromkin, V. and Rodman, R. (1978) *An Introduction to Language*. New York: Holt, Rinehart and Winston.

Greenberg. J.H. (1966) *Essays in Linguistics*. Chicago: University of Chicago Press.

Hale-Benson, J. (1994) *Unbank the Fire*. Baltimore, MD: Johns Hopkins University Press.

Hilliard, A. (1987) Testing African American students: A question of validity. A Special Issue of *The Negro Education Review*.

Hilliard, A. (1995) *The Maroon Within Us*. Publishers Group West.

Hoover, M. (1990) *Successful Black Schools*. Oakland, CA: NABRLE Publications.

O'Grady, W., Dobrovolsky, M. and Arnoff, M. (1993) *Contemporary Linguistics: An Introduction*. New York: St. Martins Press.

Ogbu, J. (1978) *Minority Education and Caste*. New York: Academic Press.

Smith, E.A. (1994) *The Historical Development of African American Language*. Los Angeles: Watts College Press.

Smitherman, G. (1994) *Black Talk*. Boston: Houghton Mifflin.

Turner, L.D. (1974) *Africanisms in the Gullah Dialect*. Ann Arbor: The University of Michigan Press.

Vass, W.K. (1979) *The Bantu Speaking Heritage of the United States*. Los Angeles: Center for Afro-American Studies, University of California, Los Angeles.

Welmers, W.E. (1973) *African Language Structures*. Berkeley, CA: University of California Press.

Williams, R.L. (1975) *Ebonics: The True Language of Black Folks*. St. Louis, MO: Institute of Black Studies.

Examples of
Legislative Reaction

CONGRESSIONAL RESPONSE

105th CONGRESS
1st Session
H. RES. 28

Expressing the sense of the House of Representatives that programs based upon the premise that 'Ebonics' is a legitimate language should not receive Federal funds.

IN THE HOUSE OF REPRESENTATIVES

Mr. KING of New York submitted the following resolution, which was referred to the Committee on Education and the Workforce

RESOLUTION

Expressing the sense of the House of Representatives that programs based upon the premise that 'Ebonics' is a legitimate language should not receive Federal funds.

Whereas 'Ebonics' is not a legitimate language: Now, therefore, be it Resolved, That it is the sense of the House of Representatives that no Federal funds should be used to pay for or support any program that is based upon the premise that 'Ebonics' is a legitimate language.

STATE REACTION:
VIRGINIA GENERAL ASSEMBLY 1997
977704140
HOUSE BILL NO. 2437

Offered January 20, 1997 A BILL to amend and reenact §§ 7.1-42 and 22.1-253.13:1 of the Code of Virginia, relating to standard English requirements.
Patron-Bryant
Referred to Committee on Education

Be it enacted by the General Assembly of Virginia:

1.   That §§ 7.1-42 and 22.1-253.13:1 of the Code of Virginia are amended and reenacted as follows:

§ 7.1-42. English designated the official language of the Commonwealth.

English shall be designated as the official language of the Commonwealth of Virginia. Except as provided by law, no state agency or local government shall be required to provide and no state agency or local government shall be prohibited from providing any documents, information, literature or other written materials in any language other than standard English. Standard English includes the written and spoken language which is accepted by generally recognized authorities as grammatically correct in the United States and shall not include any dialect, jargon, patois or vernacular based on the English language.
§ 22.1-253.13:1. Standard 1. Basic skills, selected programs, and instructional personnel.

(A) The General Assembly and the Board of Education believe that the fundamental goal of the public schools of this Commonwealth must be to enable each student to develop the skills that are necessary for success in school and preparation for life, and find that the quality of education is dependent upon the provision of the appropriate working environment, benefits, and salaries necessary to ensure the availability of high quality instructional personnel and adequate commitment of other resources.
(B) The Board of Education shall establish educational objectives to implement the development of the skills that are necessary for success in school and for preparation for life in the years beyond. The current educational objectives, known as the Standards of

Learning, shall not be construed to be regulations as defined in §9-6.14:4; however, the Board of Education may, from time to time, revise these educational objectives. In order to provide appropriate opportunity for input from the general public, teachers, and local school boards, the Board of Education shall conduct public hearings prior to establishing new educational objectives. Thirty days prior to conducting such hearings, the Board shall give written notice by mail of the date, time, and place of the hearings to all local school boards and any other persons requesting to be notified of the hearings and publish notice of its intention to revise these educational objectives in the Virginia Register of Regulations. Interested parties shall be given reasonable opportunity to be heard and present information prior to final adoption of any revisions of these educational objectives.

The Board shall, however, promulgate regulations, in compliance with §7.1-42 and in accordance with the Administrative Process Act (§9-6.14:1 et seq.), relating to the teaching of standard English and the use of any dialect, jargon, patois or vernacular in Virginia's public schools.

The Board shall seek to ensure that any revised educational objectives are consistent with the world's highest educational standards. However, no revisions shall be implemented prior to July 1, 1994. These objectives shall include, but not be limited to, basic skills of communication, computation and critical reasoning including problem solving and decision making, and the development of personal qualities such as self-esteem, sociability, self-management, integrity, and honesty. School boards shall implement these objectives or objectives specifically designed for their school divisions that are equivalent to or exceed the Board's requirements. Students shall be expected to achieve the educational objectives utilized by the school division at appropriate age or grade levels. With such funds as are available for this purpose, the Board of Education may prescribe assessment methods to determine the level of achievement of these objectives by all students.

(C) Local school boards shall develop and implement a program of instruction for grades K through 12 which emphasizes reading, writing, speaking, mathematical concepts and computations, and scientific concepts and processes; essential skills and concepts of citizenship, including knowledge of history, economics, government, foreign languages, international cultures, health, environmental issues and geography necessary for responsible participation in

American society and in the international community; fine arts and practical arts; knowledge and skills needed to qualify for further education and employment or, in the case of some handicapped children, to qualify for appropriate training; and development of the ability to apply such skills and knowledge in preparation for eventual employment and lifelong learning.

Local school boards shall also develop and implement programs of prevention, intervention, or remediation for students who are educationally at-risk including, but not limited to, those whose scores are in the bottom national quartile on Virginia State Assessment Program Tests, or who do not pass the literacy test prescribed by the Board of Education. Division superintendents may require such students to take special programs of prevention, intervention, or remediation which may include attendance in public summer school sessions, in accordance with subsection E of §22.1-254 and §22.1-254.01. Students required to attend such summer school sessions shall not be charged tuition. Based on the number of students attending and the Commonwealth's share of the per pupil costs, additional state funds shall be provided for summer remediation programs as set forth in the appropriation act.

(D) Local school boards shall also implement the following:

(1) Programs in grades K through 3 which emphasize developmentally appropriate learning to enhance success.

(2) Programs based on prevention, intervention, or retrieval designed to increase the number of students who earn a high school diploma or general education development (GED) certificate. As provided in the appropriation act, state funding, in addition to basic aid, shall be allocated to support programs grounded in sound educational policy to reduce the number of students who drop out of school. From such funds as may be appropriated for the purpose, sufficient funds shall be provided to hold all local school divisions harmless by providing no-loss funding which maintains the level of each school division's funding as allocated for drop out prevention programs on July 1, 1996, if the level of funding for such school division's drop-out prevention programs would be less than its level of funding for such programs in fiscal year 1995. Effective on and after July 1, 1996, the Board of Education shall develop and implement a funding mechanism to ensure that no school board is penalized in its state funding for drop out prevention

programs for reducing the drop out rate in its school division.

(3)   Career education programs infused into the K through 12 curricula that promote knowledge of careers and all types of employment opportunities including but not limited to, apprenticeships, the military, and career education schools, and emphasize the advantages of completing school with marketable skills. School boards may include career exploration opportunities in the middle school grades.

(4)   Competency-based vocational education programs, which integrate academic outcomes, career guidance and job-seeking skills for all secondary students including those identified as handicapped that reflect employment opportunities, labor market needs, applied basic skills, job-seeking skills, and career guidance. Career guidance shall include employment counseling designed to furnish information on available employment opportunities to all students, including those identified as handicapped, and placement services for students exiting school. Each school board shall develop and implement a plan to ensure compliance with the provisions of this subsection.

(5)   Academic and vocational preparation for students who plan to continue their education beyond secondary school or who plan to enter employment.

(6)   Early identification of handicapped students and enrollment of such students in appropriate instructional programs consistent with state and federal law.

(7)   Early identification of gifted students and enrollment of such students in appropriately differentiated instructional programs.

(8)   Educational alternatives for students whose needs are not met in programs prescribed elsewhere in these standards. Such students shall be counted in average daily membership (ADM) in accordance with the regulations of the Board of Education.

(9)   Adult education programs for individuals functioning below the high school completion level. Such programs may be conducted by the school board as the primary agency or through a collaborative arrangement between the school board and other agencies.

(10)   A plan to make achievements for students who are educa-

tionally at-risk a division wide priority which shall include procedures for measuring the progress of such students.

(E) Each local school board shall employ with state and local basic, special education, gifted, and vocational education funds a minimum number of licensed, full-time equivalent instructional personnel for each 1,000 students in average daily membership (ADM) as set forth in the appropriation act. Calculations of kindergarten positions shall be based on full-day kindergarten programs. Beginning with the March 31 report of average daily membership, those school divisions offering half-day kindergarten shall adjust their average daily membership for kindergarten to reflect eighty-five percent of the total kindergarten average daily memberships.

(F) In addition to the positions supported by basic aid and in support of regular school year remedial programs, state funding, pursuant to the appropriation act, shall be provided to fund certain full-time equivalent instructional positions for each 1,000 students in grades K through 12 estimated to score in the bottom national quartile on Virginia State Assessment Program Tests and those who fail the literacy tests prescribed by the Board. State funding for remedial programs provided pursuant to this subsection and the appropriation act may be used to support programs for educationally at-risk students as identified by the local school boards. The Board of Education shall establish criteria for identification of educationally at-risk students, which shall not be construed to be regulations as defined in §9-6.14:4; however, the Board of Education may, from time to time, revise these identification criteria. In order to provide appropriate opportunity for input from the general public, teachers, and local school boards, the Board of Education shall conduct public hearings prior to establishing or revising such identification criteria. Thirty days prior to conducting such hearings, the Board shall give written notice by mail of the date, time, and place of the hearings to all local school boards and any other persons requesting to be notified of the hearings and publish notice of its intention to establish or revise such identification criteria in the Virginia Register of Regulations. Interested parties shall be given reasonable opportunity to be heard and present information prior to final adoption of any such identification criteria or revisions thereto.

(G) Licensed instructional personnel shall be assigned by each school board in a manner that produces division wide ratios of students in average daily membership to full-time equivalent teaching positions, excluding special education teachers, principals, assistant principals, counselors, and librarians, that are not greater than the following ratios: (i) twenty-five to one in kindergarten with no class being larger than thirty students; if the average daily membership in any kindergarten class exceeds twenty-five pupils, a full-time teacher's aide shall be assigned to the class; (ii) twenty-four to one in grade one with no class being larger than thirty students; (iii) twenty-five to one in grades two and three with no class being larger than thirty students; (iv) twenty-five to one in grades four through six with no class being larger than thirty-five students; and (v) twenty-four to one in English classes in grades six through twelve.

Further, pursuant to the appropriation act, school boards may implement in kindergarten through third grade, within certain schools, lower ratios of students in average daily membership to full-time equivalent teaching positions by assigning instructional personnel in a manner that produces ratios of students in average daily membership to full-time equivalent teaching positions, excluding special education teachers, principals, assistant principals, counselors, and librarians as follows: (i) in schools having high concentrations of at-risk students, eighteen to one; and (ii) in schools having moderate concentrations of at-risk students, twenty to one. For the purposes of this subsection, "schools having high concentrations of at-risk students" and "schools having moderate concentrations of at-risk students" shall be defined in the appropriation act.

In addition, instructional personnel shall be assigned by each school board in a manner that produces school wide ratios of students in average daily memberships to full-time equivalent teaching positions of twenty-five to one in middle schools and high schools.

PROPOSED CALIFORNIA LEGISLATION AND JOHN RICKFORD'S RESPONSE

SB 205 EDUCATION: EQUALITY IN ENGLISH INSTRUCTION ACT. BILL NUMBER: SB 205 AMENDED

LEGISLATIVE COUNSEL'S DIGEST

SB 205, as amended, Haynes. Education: Equality in English Instruction Act.

Existing law requires that English be the basic language of instruction in all public schools.

This bill would enact the "Equality in English Instruction Act." The bill would require the State Department of Education to immediately terminate the Proficiency in Standard English for Speakers of Black Language program, as specified. The bill would prohibit the state, its subdivisions, and local government agencies, including school districts and community college districts, from expending state funds or resources, {+ or state-derived funds or resources, +} or applying for federal funding, for the purpose {+ or support +} of {− , or support for, the provision of Black Language, Black English, or Ebonics −} {+ nonstandard English +} instruction, as defined. The bill would require that any funding that already has been obtained for the purpose {+ or support +} of {− , or support for, the provision of Black Language, Black English, or Ebonics −} {+ nonstandard English +} instruction be instead used for the classroom teaching {− of linguistic or communication skills in the −} English {− language −}.

This bill would require the State Department of Education to submit written recommendations, within 90 days of the operative date of the bill, to the Legislature regarding the structure and implementation of a {+ proposed +} program that would provide financial incentives to school districts that, using English language instruction, improve {− linguistic or communication skills of students −} {+ the English language skill of pupils +} in low-income areas of the state and financial penalties for school districts {− where −} {+ in which +} the skills have deteriorated, as measured by objective testing data, as specified.

Vote: majority. Appropriation: no. Fiscal committee: yes. State-mandated local program: no.

SECTION 1. This act shall be known, and may be cited, as the "Equality in English Instruction Act."

SECTION 2. Section 31 is added to the Education Code to read:

31. (a) (1) It is the intent of the Legislature, in enacting the act that adds this section, that all pupils become proficient in English, regardless of race, color, sex, national origin, or other characteristic.

   (2) It is the intent of the Legislature, in enacting the act that adds this section, to eliminate specified funding sources for all nonstandard English instruction, not merely one particular class of nonstandard English instruction.

(b) For the purposes of this article, "nonstandard English" includes any of the following:

   (1) Any vernacular dialect of English.

   (2) Any language that is derived, in whole or in part, from English.

   (3) Any language that is derived, in whole or in part, from English and at least one other language.

   (4) Ebonics, Black English, Black Language, or African American Vernacular English.

   (5) Slang.

   (6) Idioms.

(c) For the purposes of this article, "nonstandard English instruction" includes any of the following:

   (1) Instruction in nonstandard English as part of a bilingual education program, as a foreign language, as a primary language, as a home language, or as a vernacular dialect.

   (2) Training teachers or administrative staff in schools to recognize, speak, write, read, or understand nonstandard English as part of a bilingual education program, as a foreign language, as a primary language, as a home language, or as a vernacular dialect.

   (3) Training teachers or administrative staff in schools to do any of the following:

      (A) Incorporate nonstandard English into their lesson plans.

      (B) Legitimize, accept, or embrace nonstandard English.

      (B) Teach that nonstandard English is a situationally correct alternative to English in *some* or all situations.

(d) Not withstanding any other provision of law:

   (1) Neither the state, nor any of its subdivisions, nor any local government agency in California, including the State Department of Education and school districts, shall utilize state funds or resources, or state-derived funds or resources, for the purpose of nonstandard English instruction or for the support of that instruction.

   (2) Any state funds or resources, or state-derived funds or resources, that have already been obtained by the state, its subdivisions, or any local government agency in California, including school districts and community college districts, for the purpose or support of nonstandard English instruction shall instead be used for the classroom teaching of English.

   (3) Neither the state, nor any of its subdivisions, nor any local government agencies in California, including school districts and community college districts, shall apply for federal funds or resources, or federal-derived funds or resources, for the purpose of nonstandard English instruction or for the support of that instruction.

(e) The State Department of Education shall immediately terminate the Proficiency in standard English for Speakers of Black Language program.

   (1) No state funds or resources, or state-derived funds or resources shall be used for, or in support of, the Proficiency in standard English for Speakers of Black Language program.

   (2) No state employee, including any person under the authority of the State Department of Education or the Superintendent of Public Instruction shall operate, support, or coordinate, or contribute to the operation, support, or coordination of the Proficiency in standard English for Speakers of Black Language program, or provide or support nonstandard English instruction, even if his or her salary is provided, in full or in part, by funds not derived from the state.

(f) Within 90 days after the operative date of the act that adds this section, the State Department of Education shall submit a written report to the Legislature regarding the structure and implementation of a proposed program that:

   (1) Provides financial incentives to school districts that, using English language instruction, improve the English language

skills of pupils in low-income areas of the state, and financial penalties for school districts in which these skills have deteriorated, as measured by objective testing data.

(2) Is funded from reading and phonics funds. + } { − cited, as the "Equality in English Instruction Act."

SECTION 2. Section 31 is added to the Education Code, to read:

31. (a) The Legislature finds and declares all of the following:

(1) The State Department of Education's Proficiency in standard English for Speakers of Black Language program distributes staff development and lesson plan materials to school districts that explicitly direct teachers to do both of the following:

(A) Incorporate slang into their lesson plans.

(B) Teach that slang is an appropriate alternative to correct English in some situations.

(2) The State Department of Education's Proficiency in standard English for Speakers of Black Language program recommends that teachers do all of the following:

(A) Advise students that using slang is more appropriate than using correct English in certain situations.

(B) "Kill the myth" that "standard English is the correct way to speak at all times."

(C) "Kill the myth" that "in order to teach standard English, the teacher must eradicate the student's home language."

(D) Speak specific sentences to their students in slang.

(E) Make audio tapes of themselves speaking in slang.

(F) Write sentences in slang on chalkboards and overhead transparencies.

(3) Granting slang an official place in California's classrooms, and directing teachers to instruct students that slang is appropriate in certain situations, legitimizes incorrect English. Legitimizing incorrect English as political correctness is a disservice to children.

(4) At least one school district has enacted, and others are contemplating enacting, policies that expand the State Department of Education's Proficiency in Standard English for Speakers of Black Language program in order to train teachers in the instructional strategies and curriculum

recommended by the State Department of Education's Black Language program.

(5) Calling their programs "Ebonics," these districts are attempting to convince students that poor communication skills are acceptable speech patterns and writing skills, and that these students cannot learn to speak correct English due to social or cultural factors outside their control. The justification for "Ebonics" instruction is the same as that used to justify separate educational institutions for African-Americans prior to the case of Brown v Board of Education. It is the perpetuation of the "separate but equal" philosophy that has harmed race relations in this country for far too many years.

(b) It is the intent of the Legislature, in enacting the act that adds this section, that every student, regardless of race, color, sex, or national origin, become proficient in correct English and obtain the linguistic and communication skills necessary to become productive members of California's communities.

(c) For the purposes of this article, "Black Language instruction," "Black English instruction," and "Ebonics instruction" shall include all of the following:

(1) The teaching in schools of what its adherents call an African-American foreign language, or a dialect unique to African-Americans, as part of a bilingual instruction program.

(2) The teaching in schools of what its adherents call an African-American foreign language, or a dialect unique to African-Americans, as a language separate and distinct from English.

(3) The training of teachers or administrative staff in schools to speak, write, read, or understand what its adherents call an African-American foreign language, or a dialect unique to African-Americans.

(4) The training of teachers or administrative staff in schools to incorporate what its adherents call an African-American foreign language, or a dialect unique to African-Americans, into their lesson plans.

(5) The training of teachers or administrative staff in schools to teach that what its adherents call an African-American foreign language, or a dialect unique to African-Americans, is an appropriate alternative to correct English in some situations.

SECTION 3. Section 32 is added to the Education Code, to read:

32. Notwithstanding any other provision of law:

(a) (1) The State Department of Education shall immediately terminate the Proficiency in standard English for Speakers of Black Language program. No state funds or resources, or state-derived funds or resources, shall be used for, or in support of, the Proficiency in standard English for Speakers of Black Language program.

   (2) No state employee, including any person under the authority of the State Department of Education or the Superintendent of Public Instruction, shall operate, support, or coordinate, or contribute to the operation, support, or coordination of the Proficiency in standard English for Speakers of Black language program, or provide or support Black Language instruction or Black English instruction or Ebonics instruction in the state of California, even if his or her salary is provided, in full or in part, by federal funds.

(b) Neither the state, nor any of its subdivisions, nor any local government agencies in California, including the State Department of Education or the Superintendent of Public Instruction, shall operate, support, or coordinate, or contribute to the operation, support or coordination of the Proficiency in standard English for speakers of Black Language program, or support Black English instruction or Ebonics instruction, shall instead be used for the classroom teaching of linguistic or communications skills solely in the English language.

(c) Neither the state, nor any of its subdivisions, nor any local government agencies in California, including school districts and community college districts, shall apply for federal funding for the purpose of, or support for, providing Black Language instruction, Black English instruction, or Ebonics instruction.

(d) Upon the operative date of the act that adds this section, any state funding that already has been obtained for the purpose of, or support for, providing Black Language instruction or Black English instruction or Ebonics instruction, shall instead be used for the classroom teaching of linguistic or communications skills solely in the English language.

(e) Within 90 days after the operative date of the act that adds this section, the State Department of Education shall submit written recommendations to the Legislature regarding the structure and implementation of a program that would accomplish each of the following:

(1) Provide financial incentives to school districts that, using English language instruction, improve the English language skills of students in low-income areas of the state, and financial penalties for school districts where these skills have deteriorated, as measured by objective testing data.

(2) Be funded from reading and phonics funds appropriated for the purpose of increasing reading, writing, or communication skill levels in the State of California. — } Searching keywords: (status am) (author Haynes) (HooS)

*Symbols and marks within this text appeared in the original.

S.B. 205 – Well-intentioned but uninformed

John R. Rickford

(Submitted to the Los Angeles Times as an Op Ed piece, March 28, 1997)

Senate Bill 205, set for hearing in the California State Senate on April 2, is a good example of how educational innovation and promise are threatened when policy makers fail to do their homework. The laudable goal of this bill, introduced by Senator Raymond Haynes (R-Riverside), is to "ensure that all pupils become proficient in English, regardless of race, color ... or other characteristic." However, the means which it proposes – immediately terminating the "standard English Proficiency" (SEP) program for speakers of Ebonics and other vernacular varieties, and preventing teachers from considering the structure of the vernacular in teaching the standard – is uninformed and misguided.

The fact of the matter is that several studies, both in the United States and from Europe, show that the goal of mastering the standard variety is more effectively achieved by approaches which take the vernacular into account than by those which ignore it or try to condemn it into nonexistence. One effective means of taking the vernacular into account is the contrastive analysis approach which is at the heart of SEP In this approach, students are explicitly taught to recognize the difference between vernacular and standard features and schooled in the standard variety through identification, translation and response drills.

Hanni Taylor, in her (1989) book, *Standard English, Black English, and Bidialectalism*, reported that a group of inner-city Aurora University students from Chicago, who were taught with contrastive analysis techniques showed a 59% REDUCTION in the use of Ebonics features in their standard English writing, while students taught by traditional methods showed an 8.5% INCREASE in the use of such features.

Henry Parker and Marilyn Crist in their (1995) book, *Teaching Minorities to Play the Corporate Language Game* also extol the virtues of the bidialectal contrastive analysis approach, which they have used successfully with vernacular speakers in Tennessee and Chicago at the preschool, elementary, high school and college levels.

The ten-year old program in De Kalb county, Georgia, where 5th and 6th grade students in eight schools are taught to switch from their "home speech" to "school speech" is another one in which contrastive analysis methods have proven effective. According to Doug Cummings (Atlanta Constitution, Jan. 9, 1997, p. B1), "The program has won a 'center of excellence' designation from the National Council for Teachers of English. Last year, students who had taken the course had improved verbal test scores at every school."

Not only would S.B. 205 rule out contrastive analysis, it would also rule out the dialect readers approach to teaching standard English via the vernacular, which has a number of striking successes to its credit (see John and Angela Rickford 1994, in Linguistics and Education 7.2).

One of the earliest dialect reader studies is Tore Osterberg, *Bilingualism and the First School Language* (1961). One group of Swedish dialect speakers was first taught to read in their vernacular, and then transitioned to standard Swedish, while another group was taught entirely in standard Swedish. After 35 weeks, the dialect method showed itself superior both in reading speed and comprehension.

Tove Bull reported on a similar study in Norway in a (1990) article (Tromsö, *Linguistics in the Eighties*). Ten classes of Norwegian first graders were taught to read and write either in their Norwegian vernaculars or standard Norwegian. Bull's results were similar to Osterberg's: "the vernacular children read significantly faster and better ... particularly the less bright children" (p. 78).

The most similar U.S. experiment was the Bridge readers co-authored by Gary Simpkins, Grace Holt, and Charlesetta Simpkins in 1977 (Houghton Mifflin). These provided reading materials in Ebonics, a transitional variety, and standard English. The 417 students across the United States taught with Bridge showed an average reading gain of 6.2 months over 4 months of instruction, while the 123 taught by regular methods gained only 1.6 months – showing the same below par progress which leads African American and other dialect speakers to fall further and further behind. Despite their dramatic success, the Bridge readers were discontinued because of hostile, uninformed reactions to the recognition of the vernacular in the classroom. William Stewart and Joan Baratz's promising attempts to introduce dialect readers in a school in Washington DC in 1969 were similarly squelched.

Let us hope that the attempt of Oakland, Los Angeles and other California school districts to use contrastive analysis within the SEP as a strategy for teaching standard English does not meet a similar fate via S.B. 205. Although contrastive analysis and dialect readers are not the only viable approaches to teaching the standard, these innovative methods do work. And school districts attempting to reverse their devastating failure rates with inner city African Americans and other dialect speakers should not be hamstrung by policy makers who may be well-intentioned but are decidedly uninformed.

(John R. Rickford is Professor of Linguistics at Stanford University. He is currently co-authoring a book on African American Vernacular English for Cambridge University Press, and co-editing another on African American English for Routledge.)

Legal
Background

MARTIN LUTHER KING JUNIOR ELEMENTARY SCHOOL CHILDREN ET AL. V. ANN ARBOR SCHOOL DISTRICT BOARD

473 F. Supp. 1371 (1979)

Memorandum Opinion and Order, Joiner, District Judge

The issue before this court is whether the defendant School Board has violated Section 1703(f) of Title 20 of the United States Code as its actions relate to the 11 black children who are plaintiffs in this case and who are students in the Martin Luther King Junior Elementary School operated by the defendant School Board. It is alleged that the children speak a version of "black English," "black vernacular" or "black dialect" as their home and community language that impedes their equal participation in the instructional programs, and that the school has not taken appropriate action to overcome the barrier.

A major goal of American education in general, and of King School in particular, is to train young people to communicate both orally (speaking and understanding oral speech) and in writing (reading and understanding the written word and writing so that others can understand it) in the standard vernacular of society. The art of communication among the people of the country in all aspects of people's lives is a basic building block in the development of each individual. Children need to learn to speak and understand and to read and write the language used by society to carry on its business, to develop its science, arts and culture, and to carry on its professions and governmental functions. Therefore, a major goal of a school system is to teach reading, writing, speaking and understanding standard English.

The problem in this case revolves around the ability of the school system, King School in particular, to teach the reading of standard English to children who, it is alleged, speak "black English" as a matter of course at home and in their home community (the Green Road Housing Development).

This case is not an effort on the part of the plaintiffs to require that they be taught "black English" or that their instruction throughout their schooling be in "black English," or that a dual language program be provided... It is a straightforward effort to require the court to intervene on the children's behalf to require the defendant School District Board to take appropriate action to teach them to read in the standard English of the school, the commercial world, the arts, science and professions. This action is a cry for judicial help in opening the doors to the establishment... to keep another generation from becoming functionally illiterate.

The court heard from a number of distinguished and renowned researchers and professionals who testified as to the existence of a language system, which is a part of the English language but different in significant respects from the standard English used in the school setting, the commercial world, the world of the arts and science, among the professions and in government. It is and has been used at some time by 80% of the black people of this country and has as its genesis the transactional or pidgin language of the slaves, which after a generation or two became a Creole language. It still flourishes in areas where there are concentrations of black people. It contains aspects of southern dialect and is used largely by black people in their casual conversation and informal talk... The experts further testified, however, that efforts to instruct the children in standard English by teachers who failed to appreciate that the children speak a dialect which is acceptable in the home and peer community can result in the children becoming ashamed of their language, and thus impede the learning process. In this respect, the black dialect appears to be different than the usual foreign languages because a foreign language is not looked down on by the teachers. The evidence also suggests that there are fewer reading role models among the poor black families than among families in the rest of society.

Finally, it is clear that black children who succeed, and many do, learn to be bilingual. They retain fluency in "black English" to maintain status in the community and they become fluent in standard English to succeed in the general society. They achieve in this way by learning to "code switch" from one to the other depending on the circumstances.

A child who does not learn to read is impeded in equal participation in the educational programs. Such a child cannot fully participate in the educational programs which to a significant degree require the student to acquire knowledge from the written word. Reading of all kinds is a major method by which modern society passes on its information and culture among its members and to its children. It is the way in which society conveys its commands and gives direction to its members.

The research evidence supports the theory that the learning of reading can be hurt by teachers who reject students because of the "mistakes" or "errors" made in oral speech by "black English" speaking children who are learning standard English. This comes about because "black English" is commonly thought of as an inferior method of speech and those who use this system may be thought of as "dumb" or "inferior." The child who comes to school using the "black English" system of communication and who is taught that this is wrong loses a sense of values related to mother and close friends and siblings and may rebel at efforts by his teachers to teach reading in a different language...

If a barrier exists because of the language used by the children in this case, it exists not because the teachers and students cannot understand each other, but because in the process of attempting to teach the students how to speak standard English the students are made somehow to feel inferior and are thereby turned off from the learning process.

There is no direct evidence that any of the teachers in this case has treated the home language of the children as inferior, but... [T]he teachers do not... admit to taking that system into account in helping the student read standard English. The evidence... suggests that the students... communicate orally quite well in standard English... however... these children have not developed reading skills and the failure to develop these skills impedes equal participation in the instructional program.

The court cannot find that the defendant School Board has taken steps (1) to help the teachers understand the problem; (2) to help provide them with knowledge about the children's use of a "black English" language system; and (3) to suggest ways and means of using that knowledge in teaching the students to read...

[T]he evidence suggests clearly that no matter how well intentioned the teachers are, they are not likely to be successful in overcoming the language barrier caused by their failure to take into account the home language system, unless they are helped by the defendant to recognize the existence of the language system used by the children in their home community and to use that knowledge as a way of helping the children to learn to read standard English.

Counsel for the defendant is directed to submit to this court within thirty (30) days a proposed plan defining the exact steps to be taken (1) to help the teachers of the plaintiff children at King School to identify children speaking "black English" as the language spoken as a home or community language, and (2) to use that knowledge in teaching such students how to read standard English. The plan must embrace within its terms the elementary school teachers of the plaintiff children at Martin Luther King Junior Elementary School. If the defendant chooses, however, it may submit a broader plan for the court's consideration, e.g. one embracing other elementary schools.

So ordered.

Linguists'
Reactions

A Linguist Looks At the Ebonics Debate[1]

CHARLES J. FILLMORE
University of California, Berkeley

One uncontroversial principle underlying the Oakland Unified School District's December 18th "Ebonics" resolution is the truism that people can't learn from each other if they don't speak the same language. Anyone who doubts this has only to read the current public debate about the resolution itself. Educators, bureaucrats, and experts have been weighing in on the meaning of the resolution in the last two weeks. You might think all that these people speak the same language, but the evidence contradicts the appearance. All of the key words that keep coming up in these discussions clearly mean different things to different parties in the debate, and that blocks successful communication and makes it too easy for each participant to believe that the others are mad, scheming, or stupid.

As far as I can work it out (not from the language of the resolution but from the board's recent "clarifications"), the pedagogically relevant assumptions behind the "Ebonics" resolution are as follows: The way some African American children speak when they show up in Oakland's schools is so different from standard English that teachers often can't understand what they are saying. Such children perform poorly in school and typically fail to acquire the ways of speaking that they'll need in order to succeed in the world outside their neighborhoods. Schools have traditionally treated the speech of these children as simply sloppy and wrong, not as evidencing skills and knowledge the children can build on. The proposed new instructional plan would assist children in learning standard English by encouraging them to compare the way they speak with what they need to learn in school, and this cannot be accomplished in a calm and reasoned way unless their teachers treat what they already have, linguistically, as a worthy possession rather than as evidence of carelessness and ignorance. An important step toward introducing this

161

new practice is to help teachers understand the characteristics of their students' speech so they can lead the children to an awareness of the difference.

It would have been more natural for me to describe the plan with such words as "building on the language the children already have to help them acquire the language they need to learn in school." But instead, I avoided using the word "language," since that is one of the words responsible for much of the confusion in the discussion around the school board's decision. The other words causing trouble are "dialect," "slang," "primary language," and, regrettably, "genetic." Neither side in these debates uses these words in ways that facilitate communication. Perhaps a linguist's view might introduce some clarity into these discussions.

The words "dialect" and "language" are confusingly ambiguous. These are not precisely definable technical terms in linguistics, but linguists have learned to live with the ambiguities. I mentioned "the language of the resolution" where I meant the actual words and phrases found in the text of the board's resolution. We can use the word "language" to refer simply to the linguistic system one acquires in childhood. In normal contexts, everybody grows up speaking a language. And if there are systematic differences between the language you and your neighbors speak and the language my neighbors and I speak, we can say that we speak different dialects.

The word "language" is also used to refer to a group of related dialects, but there are no scientific criteria for deciding when to refer to two linguistic systems as different dialects of the same language, or as different languages belonging to the same language family. There are empirical criteria for grouping ways of speaking to reflect their historical relationships, but there is an arbitrary element in deciding when to use the word "language" for representing any particular grouping. (Deciding whether BBC newsreaders and Lynchburg, VA radio evangelists speak different dialects of the same language or different languages in the same language family is on the level of deciding whether Greenland is a small continent or a large island).

There is a different and misleading way of using these words for situations in which, for social or political reasons, one dialect comes to be the preferred means of communication in schools, commerce, public ceremonies, etc. According to this second usage, which reflects an unscientific "folk theory" what the linguist would simply call the standard dialect is thought of as a "language," the others as "mere dialects," falling short of the perfection of the real language. An important principle of linguistics is that the selection of the prestige dialect is determined by accidental extralinguistic forces, and is not dependent on inherent virtues of the dialects themselves. But according to the folk theory, the "dialects" differ from the language itself in being full of errors.

I've been reading the San Francisco newspapers these last two weeks, and I see continuing chaos in the ways commentators choose to describe and classify the manner of speaking that is the target of the Ebonics resolution. The resolution and the public discussion about it have used so many different terms, each of them politically loaded ("Ebonics," "Black English," "Black Dialect," "African Language Systems," "Pan-African Communication Behaviors") that I will use what I think is the most neutral term, "African American Vernacular English," abbreviated as AAVE.

(1) Some participants in this debate think that AAVE is merely an imperfectly learned approximation to real English, differing from it because the speakers are careless and lazy and don't follow "the rules." It is "dialect," in the deprecating use of that word, or "slang."

(2) To most linguists AAVE is one of the dialects of American English, historically most closely related to forms of Southern speech but with differences attributable both to the linguistic history of slaves and to generations of social isolation. (For a linguist, to describe something as a dialect is not to say that it is inferior; everybody speaks a dialect.)

(3) And some people say that while AAVE has the superficial trappings of English, at its structural core it is a continuation or amalgam of one or more west African languages.

The views summarized in (1) are simply wrong. The difference between the views identified in (2) and (3) is irrelevant to the issue the board is trying to face.

The Oakland resolution asks that the schools acknowledge that AAVE is the "primary language" of many of the children who enter Oakland schools. What this means is that it is their home language, the form of speech the children operated in during the first four or five years of their lives, the language they use with their family and friends. An early explanation of the purpose of the new program (*San Francisco Chronicle* 12/20) is that it "is intended to help teachers show children how to translate their words from 'home language' to the 'language of wider communication.'"

Understanding this as the meaning of the phrase, it makes sense to ask if something is or is not some particular person's "primary language," but the simple question of whether something is or isn't "a primary language" is incoherent. The people who have expressed such concerns clearly think the term means something other than what I think the school board intended.

The *Chronicle* (12/20) asked readers to send in their opinions "on the Oakland school board's decision to recognize Ebonics, or black English, as a primary language." *The San Francisco Examiner* (12/20) attributed to Delaine Eastin, state Superintendent of Public Instruction, the worry that the decision to "recognize" AAVE could lead students to believe "that they could prosper with it as their primary language outside the home." An *Examiner* writer editorialized (12/20) that "[i]n the real world of colleges and commerce and communication, it's not OK to speak Ebonics as a primary language. Job recruiters don't bring along a translator." The *Chronicle* (12/24) accounts for Oakland's sudden fame as happening "all because the school board voted to treat black English like any other primary language spoken by students."

These commentators were clearly not worried about whether there really are people who have AAVE as their primary language. They all seem to understand the term "primary language" in some different way. Perhaps the term "home language" wouldn't have created so much misunderstanding.

The critics have also worried about whether AAVE "is a language." One way of understanding the question is whether it is a language rather than a mere collection of "mistakes." This seems to be the way Ward Connerly understands the question, and his answer is that it isn't a language. Another is whether it has the full status of a language rather than a dialect, in the folk use of these words mentioned above. This seems to be the view attributed to James Baldwin, in a 1979 article quoted by Pamela Budman, 12/26. Baldwin thought it "patronizing" to speak of AAVE as a dialect rather than as a full-fledged language.

But on the question of whether there is a definable linguistic system, spoken by many African Americans, with its own phonology, lexicon and grammar (and dialects!), there is already a huge body of research. (For a useful bibliography see the web site http://www2.colgate.edu/ diw/SOAN244bibs.html). The question of whether twenty-seven thousand African American children in Oakland schools come from families that speak that language has to be an empirical question, not an issue for tapping people's opinions.

The *Chronicle* (12/20) reports the nation's shock at the news of the resolution by "the Oakland school district's decision to recognize the African American vernacular as a language." Under the headline "Ebonics Isn't a Language" in the *Examiner* (12/25), Education Secretary Riley is reported as warning about the dangers of "[e]llevating black English to the status of a language."

When the *Examiner* issued its invitation for readers' opinions (12/23) the phrasing was: "Will recognition of black English as a language help African-American students succeed?" Some readers might have understood "recognition... as a language" as involving whether there is such a language at all, others as whether it is a language separate from English in the way that French and Hausa are, and still others as whether Oakland was proposing that AAVE join standard English as one of the languages to be used in the city's classrooms. It is amazing to me that the issue was thought of as deserving treatment as a yes-or-no question. It is even more amazing that so many readers felt they were qualified to answer the question.

One of the claims contained in the resolution is that Ebonics is not a linguistic cousin of English, but is really more directly descended from West African linguistic stock. (Though one Oakland teacher was heard on national TV as saying that Ebonics is basically Swahili.) Raising this issue has really muddied the pedagogical problem the schools are facing. Instead of focusing on the cognitive consequences in American schools of students' having AAVE as their primary language, whatever its source or status, the board chose to confuse the world with an irrelevant claim about language classification.

A *Chronicle* editorial (12/20) after surveying what it described as AAVE features, stated that "Such variations amount to a dialect of English – not a separate language." My Berkeley colleague, John McWhorter, was quoted (Chronicle 12/21) as saying, "Black English is a dialect – it is not a separate language." Here I am sure that he meant that it is a dialect of English.

The *Examiner* (12/24) referred to the School District's attempts to explain "its decision to adopt black English as a separate language" but the next day (12/25) quoted board member Jean Quan as saying, "We never said it was a separate language." What turns on the answer to this question? One possibility is that if AAVE can be recognized as something other than a variety of English, that fact should allow the school district to qualify for funds earmarked for bilingual education. Whether or not this was the intention of the board, it is certainly true that many people assumed that it was. An early report in the *Chronicle* (12/20) stated quite straightforwardly that "[t]he educators hope to win federal bilingual dollars to help pay for the program." On the next day the *Chronicle* added: "Education officials in some districts, including San Francisco and Los Angeles, say they are intrigued with what Oakland did and might do the same – primarily to seek federal bilingual education funds." San Francisco school board member Dan Kelly too "would support a move to have the federal government recognize Ebonics as a separate language for purposes of funding bilingual education." Whatever the intentions of the board might have been, observers across the nation read a local policy decision urging the recognition of AAVE as the home language of many students as a step in justifying a request for federal funding. (A *Chicago Tribune* editorial, quoted in the *Chronicle* 12/28, assumed that giving AAVE "the status of a language" would entail "qualify[ing] the children who speak it to receive federally funded bilingual education.")

The intentions regarding funding are somewhat unclear, but the resolution did suggest that they intended to use AAVE as a language of instruction. Explaining things to children in a language they understand is one thing; teaching that language to the children is something else, and this is the possibility that raised some alarms.

The resolution declares that "the Superintendent in conjunction with her staff shall devise and implement the best possible academic program for imparting instruction to African American students in their primary language for the combined purposes of maintaining the legitimacy and richness of such language... and to facilitate their acquisition and mastery of English language skills." Here the source of ambiguity is the word "maintaining": it could refer to defending the belief that the language is legitimate and rich, or it could refer to preserving the language from decline. The second (and I would suspect unintended) interpretation is the one that led some people to think that the district intended to offer classes in AAVE. (A belief that this is what they meant led Jesse Jackson to say that children would be better off studying Spanish.)

To resolve these various misunderstandings, the board has hired the PR firm of Darolyn Davis, whose job, according to the *Chronicle* (12/24) is "to help them explain that they have no intention of teaching children to speak black English – Ebonics – or applying for federal bilingual dollars to their program under false pretenses." This has been done in the form of a statement of "legislative intent."

The questions until now have been: "is it a primary language?"; "is it a language?"; and "is it a separate language?" The next word to worry about is whether AAVE is simply "slang." This term is usually used to refer to ephemeral faddish locutions usually associated with schools, sports, music and entertainment, and gang life, existing mainly for expressing group solidarity, especially among the young and hip. But it has been one of the favorite dismissing words of the critics of the school board's actions. Jesse Jackson is quoted in the *Examiner* (12/22) as saying, "In Oakland some madness has erupted over making slang talk a second language." To which he added, "You don't have to go to school to learn to talk garbage."

The *Chronicle* reported (12/21) that "[s]ome scholars call it slang, criticizing Oakland for legitimizing error-ridden speech." ("Some scholars?" What are these people scholars of, if they can decide that something is slang?) We learn that in addition to the Rev. Jackson, Ward Connerly calls it slang, and complains that the board's action will "legitimize" it. Shelby Steele (*Chronicle*, 12/20) calls black English "merely slang." Listeners to talk shows (*Chronicle*, 12/21) learn "that Oakland is giving up on conventional English and diverting black kids into classes taught in slang." A Debra Saunders piece (*Chronicle*, 12/24) writes that black parents "may not welcome a philosophy that elevates slang." All of these quotations suggest that their authors do not believe that there exists anything deserving to be treated as an actual linguistic system in the speech of the students in question. The most stunning such judgment comes from Ward Connerly (*Chronicle*, 12/21): "These are kids that have had every opportunity to acclimate themselves to American society, and they have gotten themselves into this trap of speaking this language – this slang, really – that people can't understand. Now we're going to legitimize it." Mr. Connerly seems not to believe that the children in question have acquired a way of speaking through the normal process of language acquisition.

The most controversial paragraph of the resolution introduced the word "genetics" into the debate. It is really difficult to know what the writers of the phrase had in mind. In the language of the resolution, "numerous validated studies" have demonstrated "that African Language Systems are genetically based and not a dialect of English."

This passage was interpreted by many as claiming that Black English is biologically innate in its speakers. Now there is a metaphorical linguistic concept of "genetic" relationships, as when we say that Spanish and Italian are genetically related to Latin, but neither the language of the resolution nor the board's later clarifications have brought their usage any closer to the linguistic notion.

The board has since explained (*Chronicle*, 12/25) that they were not claiming "that black people have a unique biology" but merely

(*Examiner*, 12/22) that AAVE has a "historical and cultural basis." A clarification appearing on the OUSD's web page states that "[t]he term 'genetically based' is a synonym with genesis... used according to the standard dictionary definition of 'has its origins in,' It is not used to refer to human biology." There is no easy way to substitute either "genesis" or "has its origins in" into the phrasing of the resolution and come up with something coherent. In the first place, something is missing: what would follow the "in" of "has its origins in?"

The efforts to explain the bit about genetics have not been effective. As late as December 31, we read Clyde Haberman in the *New York Times* challenging the board to explain the graceful English of the Ghanaian Kofi Annan, the new United Nations Secretary General. The implication is that Kofi Annan's genes clearly didn't destine him to be a speaker of AAVE.

There is a common-sense core to the Oakland school board's plans. All over the world children show up in school speaking a variety of language that differs in some great or small way from the variety they're about to start learning. Where the discrepancy is slight, and where (as in most parts of the world) nobody would think of telling the children to give up their home language, the difference can be easily bridged. But in all cases it is natural for teachers to do whatever they can to make students aware of the differences.

The case made by the board is that this bridging from the home language to the school language should be done in a way that isn't demeaning to the children. Such elementary concern for the children's self-esteem has been ridiculed by some as a meaningless gesture of "political correctness," and a belief that children should never be corrected. But clearly, a child who can say freely, "In my dialect we say it like this" is better able to profit from a language-learning experience than a child who is simply always told that everything he says is "wrong." (And is anybody thinking about the parents of AAVE-speaking children who have been listening to all this talk about "garbage" and "nonsense"?)

The language used by the Oakland school board in formulating the resolution has occasioned great and continuing misunderstandings, leading to worries about whether the city of Oakland's reputation has been so seriously damaged that employers will stay away. Yet board members, insisting that they will never modify the language of the resolution, have instead hired a PR firm to help them justify the language they already have.

I think the board should practice what they preach and should do what they say they want their students to do: learn the language of the larger community so that they can achieve their goals in that community. Why not start over with the language of the resolution? And maybe in the work of changing the way they communicate what they originally wanted to say, they might even consider making some changes in what it was that they originally wanted to say.

In the board's public statements they should show a clearer understanding of what they are getting into. The changes needed will not be trivial, and will have to include the daunting job of sensitizing teachers to a language many of them have wanted to believe does not exist. Much of the public debate suggests that the new classroom practice will be mostly a matter of displaying respect for the children's home language, and making students aware of the pronunciation of "with" as "wif," the uses of "be," and multiple negation. But anybody who has looked at the linguistic structure of the African American vernacular knows that there's a lot more to it than that.

The OUSD school board has made an important proposal: that the work of helping speakers of black English to learn the language of the school will be easier and more effective if it is seen as building on a home language whose properties the children are encouraged to examine, rather than as an endless process of "correcting mistakes." If that's all the new policy achieves, it will have been worth it. If teachers can attain precise understandings of the nature of that language, that will be even better. If all of this discussion encourages everyone involved to make whatever other changes need to be made to improve the school performance of African American students in the district, Oakland will achieve a new and more welcome kind of fame.

January, 1997
Charles J. Fillmore is professor of Linguistics at the University of California, Berkeley.

Note

1. © Center for Applied Linguistics (www.cal.org). Revised: 4/17/97. For more information contact carolyn@cal.org. Reprinted with permission.

Ebonics and Linguistic Science: Clarifying the Issues[1]

WALT WOLFRAM
North Carolina State University

1. Issues Framing the Oakland Ebonics Controversy

- Underlying socio-educational and political issues
- Facts and fantasies about dialect diversity
- The challenge for (socio)linguistic education

2. The Role of Social Scientists in Public Affairs (Rickford, 1997)

Principle of Error Correction

A scientist who becomes aware of a widespread idea or social practice with important consequences that is invalidated by his [sic] own data is obligated to bring this error to the attention of the widest possible audience. (Labov, 1982, p. 172)

Principle of the Debt Incurred

An investigator who has obtained linguistic data from members of a speech community has an obligation to use the knowledge based on that data for the benefit of the community, when it has need of it. (Labov, 1982, p. 173)

Principle of Linguistic Gratuity

Investigators who have obtained linguistic data from members of a speech community should actively pursue ways in which they can return linguistic favors to the community. (Wolfram, 1993, p. 227)

3. Synopsis of Resolution:

On December 18, 1996, the Oakland Unified School District Board of Education approved a policy affirming Standard American English development for all students. The policy mandates that effective instructional strategies must be utilized in order to ensure that every child has the opportunity to achieve English language proficiency. Language development for African American students, who comprise 53% of the students in the Oakland schools, will be enhanced with the recognition and understanding of the language structures unique to African American students. This language has been studied for several decades and is variously referred to as Ebonics (literally "Black sounds"), or "Pan-African Communication Behaviors," or African Language Systems." Most linguists, black and white, still prefer the term "African American Vernacular English" (AAVE) to the term "Ebonics" and other alternative terms for the variety referred to in the resolution. However, the label has nothing to do with the linguistic status of the language variety (Oakland Unified School District's "Synopsis of the Adopted Policy on Standard American English Development").

4. Some Statements and Issues Generating a Controversial Media Event

- **The Separate Language Issue Resolution Statement**: "African Language Systems have origins in West and Niger-Congo [African] languages and are not merely dialects of English."
  Popular Interpretation: Ebonics is a separate language.
  Linguistic Understanding: Language varieties may be comprised of components from different languages and dialects of English; language and dialect exist on a continuum.
- **The African Base Issue Resolution Statement**: "...recognizes the existence and the cultural and historic bases of West and Niger-Congo African Language Systems, and these are the language patterns that many African American students bring to school"
  Popular Interpretation: Ebonics is an African language.
  Linguistic Understanding: Language varieties may fuse different language donor sources in the formation of a distinct variety; this is natural and widespread. One hypothesis on the origin of African American English posits a link with creoles found in the African diaspora (e.g. Sierra Leone Krio, Jamaican Creole, Gullah).
- **The Genetic Issue Resolution Statement**: "African Language Systems are genetically based and not a dialect of English." (in December 18 resolution only)
  Popular Interpretation: African Americans are biologically predisposed towards a particular language.
  Linguistic Understanding: "Genetic" in the study of historical linguistics refers to linguistic origins, not biological predisposition.

For example, one might say that German and English are genetically related because they come from the same historical source, or "language family."

- **The Bilingual Issue Resolution Statement:** "the English language acquisition and improvement skills of African-American students are as fundamental as is application of bilingual or second language learner principles for others whose primary languages are other than English."

    Popular Interpretation: Speakers of Ebonics should qualify for federally funded programs restricted to bilingual populations, for example, Spanish-English bilingual programs.

    Linguistic Understanding: Speakers of varieties other than standard English should have access to programs where they can learn standard English; it is advantageous for such programs to take into account the systematic differences of the native language variety.

- **The Teaching Issue Resolution Statement:** ". . . implement the best possible academic program for the combined purposes of facilitating the acquisition of and mastery of English language skills, while respecting and embracing the legitimacy and richness of the language patterns whether they are known as 'Ebonics,' 'African Language Systems,' 'Pan African Communication Behaviors,' or other description."

    Popular Interpretation: Students will be taught in Ebonics and teachers will be taught to use Ebonics in instruction.

    Linguistic Understanding: Students' community dialects will be respected and affirmed in the teaching process, and standard English will be used as the medium of instruction for schools.

5. The Linguistic Society of America Resolution on the Oakland Ebonics Issue

Whereas there has been a great deal of discussion in the media and among the American public about the 18 December 1996 decision of the Oakland School Board to recognize the language variety spoken by many African American students and to take it into account in teaching standard English, the Linguistic Society of America, as a society of scholars engaged in the scientific study of language, hereby resolves to make it known that:

(a) The variety known as "Ebonics," "African American Vernacular English" (AAVE), and "Vernacular Black English" and by other names is systematic and rule-governed like all natural speech varieties. In fact, all human linguistic systems-spoken, signed, and written-are fundamentally regular. The systematic and expressive nature of the grammar and pronunciation patterns of the African American vernacular has been established by numerous scientific studies over the past thirty years. Characterizations of Ebonics as "slang," "mutant," "lazy," "defective;" "ungrammatical," or "broken English" are incorrect and demeaning.

(b) The distinction between "languages" and "dialects" is usually made more on social and political grounds than on purely linguistic ones. For example, different varieties of Chinese are popularly regarded as "dialects," though their speakers cannot understand each other, but speakers of Swedish and Norwegian, which are regarded as separate "languages," generally understand each other. What is important from a linguistic and educational point of view is not whether AAVE is called a "language" or a "dialect" but rather that its systematic be recognized.

(c) As affirmed in the LSA Statement of Language Rights (June 1996), there are individual and group benefits to maintaining vernacular speech varieties and there are scientific and human advantages to linguistic diversity. For those living in the United States there are also benefits in acquiring standard English and resources should be made available to all who aspire to mastery of standard English. The Oakland School Board's commitment to helping students master standard English is commendable.

(d) There is evidence from Sweden, the U.S., and other countries that speakers of other varieties can be aided in their learning of the standard variety by pedagogical approaches which recognize the legitimacy of the other varieties of a language. From this perspective, the Oakland School Board's decision to recognize the vernacular of African American students in teaching them standard English is linguistically and pedagogically sound.

Chicago, Illinois
January 1997

6. Some Real Linguistic Issues Related to the Current Study of African American Vernacular English (from Wolfram, 1991, p. 106–116)

- The relationship between African American and Anglo American Vernacular varieties e.g. same or different, how different, distance from standard, etc.

- The origin of African American Vernacular English e.g. the Creolist (derived from a creole predecessor) vs. the Anglicist hypothesis (derived from British dialects)
- The direction of change in African American Vernacular English e.g. present day divergence vs. convergence, historical shifts, change in relation to surrounding varieties of English

7. Rationale for Dialect Awareness Programs in American Education

- The humanistic rationale
- The equity rationale
- The scientific rationale
- The socio-historical rationale
- The utilitarian rationale

8. An Example of Systematic Dialect Patterning: Dialect Study as Scientific inquiry (from Wolfram *et al.*, 1996)

In some dialects of English, some words that end in -ing can take an a-, pronounced as uh, in front of the word. Try to figure out this rule in several steps by looking at the kinds of -ing words can and cannot attach to. Do this by appealing to inner feelings, or intuitions, about the sentence pairs.

Look at the sentence pairs in LIST A and decide which sentence in each pair sounds better for attaching the a-. For example, in the first sentence pair, does it sound better to say, "A-building is hard work" or "He was a-building a house?" For each sentence pair, just choose one sentence that sounds better with the a-.

LIST A: Sentence Pairs for A- Prefixing

1. a. ___ Building is hard work.
    b. ___ She was building a house.

2. a. ___ He likes hunting.
    b. ___ He went hunting.

3. a. ___ The child was charming the adults.
    b. ___ The child was very charming.

4. a. ___ The speaker was shocking the audience with her stories.
    b. ___ The story was shocking.

5. a. ___ They thought fishing was easy.
   b. ___ They were fishing this morning.

6. a. ___ The fishing is still good here.
   b. ___ They go fishing less now.

Examine each of the sentence pairs in terms of the choices for the a-prefix and answer the following questions. The first step in figuring out the pattern for a- prefix is related to the part of speech of the -ing word. Now let's look at another difference related to prepositions such as from and by. Based on the sentence pairs in LIST B, say whether or not the a-form can be used after a preposition. Use the same technique you used for LIST A. Select the sentence that sounds better for each sentence pair and say whether it is the sentence with or without the preposition.

LIST B: A Further Detail for A- Patterning

1. a. ___ They make money by building houses.
   b. ___ They make money building houses.

2. a. ___ People can't make enough money fishing.
   b. ___ People can't make enough money from fishing.

3. a. ___ People destroy the beauty of the island through littering.
   b. ___ People destroy the beauty of the island littering.

We now have another detail for figuring the pattern for the a- prefix use related to prepositions. But there is still another part to the pattern for a- prefix use. This time, however, it is related to pronunciation. For the following -ing words, try to figure out what it is about the pronunciation that makes one sentence sound better than the other. To help you figure out the pronunciation trait that is critical for this pattern, the stressed or accented syllable of each word is marked with the symbol '. Follow the same procedure that you did in choosing the sentence in each sentence pair that sounds better.

LIST C: Figuring Out a Pronunciation Pattern for A- Prefix

1. a. ___ She was discovering a trail.
   b. ___ She was following a trail.

2. a. ___ She was repeating the chant.
    b. ___ She was hollering the chant.

3. a. ___ They were figuring the change.
    b. ___ They were forgetting the change.

4. a. ___ The baby was recognizing the mother.
    b. ___ The baby was wrecking everything.

5. a. ___ The were decorating the room.
    b. ___ They were demanding more time off.

Say exactly how the pattern for attaching the a- prefix works. Be sure to include the three different details from your examination of the examples in LISTS A, B, and C.

In LIST D, identify which of the sentences may attach an a- prefix and which may not. Use your understanding of the rule to explain why the -ing form may or may not take the a- prefix.

LIST D: Applying the A- Prefix Rule

1. She kept handing me more work.
2. The team was remembering the game.
3. The team won by playing great defense.
4. The team was playing real hard.
5. The coach was charming.

9. Systematicity in Ebonics: The Case of Habitual BE

The form *be* in African American Vernacular English refers to an action that takes place lots of times. It does not usually refer to an action that takes place only once. This is the reason that be sounds better in a sentence like "They usually be tired when they come home" than it does in a sentence like "They be tired right now." In the following sentences, this dialect pattern is shown in italics, along with responses from a sample of African American sixth grade children.

Number of People Who Choose Answer

(1) (32) a. They usually *be* tired when they come home.
    (3) b. They *be* tired right now.

(2) (31) a. When we play basketball, she be on my team.
     (4) b. The girl in the picture be my sister.

(3) (4) a. James be coming to school right now.
     (31) b. James always be coming to school.

(4) (24) a. Wanda be going to school every day.
     (11) b. Wanda be in school today.

(5) (3) a. My ankle be broken from the fall.
     (32) b. Sometimes my ears be itching.

References

Labov, W. (1982) Objectivity and commitment in linguistic science. *Language in Society* 11, 165–211.
Rickford, J. (1997) Unequal partnership: Sociolinguistics and the African American speech community. *Language in Society* 26 (2), 161–197.
Wolfram, W. (1993) Ethical considerations in language awareness programs. *Issues in Applied Linguistics* 4, 225–255.
Wolfram, W. (1991) *Dialects and American English*. Englewood Cliffs, NJ: Prentice Hall.
Wolfram, W., Schilling-Estes, N. and Hazen, K. (1996) *Dialects and the Ocracoke Brogue. 8th Grade Curriculum*. Raleigh, NC: North Carolina Language and Life Project.

Note
1. © Center for Applied Linguistics (www.cal.org). Originally published 1/30/97, revised 4/17/97. For more information contact carolyn@cal.org. Reprinted with permission.

Dialect Readers Revisited[1]

JOHN R. RICKFORD and ANGELA E. RICKFORD

Summary

Research on AAVE conducted during the 1960s was primarily concerned with developing improved methods of teaching reading and the language arts to African American children in the inner cities. The seminal work on dialect readers was summarized in a collection, *Teaching Black Children to Read* (1969), which set the stage for producing reading materials in the AAVE dialect. The 1970s saw some materials development, the most ambitious of which was the Bridge reading program developed by Simpkins et al. (1977). Although experimental efforts have been limited, there seemed to be good and positive evidence to bolster the tenet that these readers are effective in helping students bridge the gap from dialect to standard English use. None of the efforts lasted long, mainly because there was a negative reaction to using the readers, mainly by parents and educators, causing linguists to also reject dialect readers as a "solution to the reading problems of vernacular-speaking African American youth" (p. 114).

The authors argue for continued experimental research on the effectiveness of dialect readers, along with research on the attitudes in the community. They report on some newer work in the form of three "ministudies" conducted with students and teachers in the San Francisco Bay area. Elementary and middle school students and teachers were presented with two stories from the Bridge series and asked to respond to them. The students in general, but not necessarily across the board, preferred the AAVE stories and did considerably better in answering questions about the texts written in the dialect. Teachers' responses were mixed, in general tending to prefer the standard English versions. Quotes from students and educators in the article point to the fact that there is a great deal of merit in pursuing research in classrooms where there are significant numbers in schools with substantial African American populations.

The authors make some recommendations about dialect readers in light of the fact that reading problems by AAVE speakers persist, indeed have been "exacerbat[ed]" (p. 121). Prior research has provided some clear lessons learned that need to be taken into account if dialect readers are to enter the educational picture again (pp. 121–122).

- New, updated dialect readers are needed, along with "corresponding standard English (SE) texts which are carefully matched to the dialect texts in terms of readability and grade level,... difficulty of comprehension and... exercises."
- "Participants who receive the AAVE and SE versions of the same narrative [need to be] comparable in terms of reading ability and... evenly divided along gender lines."
- There is a need to do a combination of short-term and long-term studies with elementary and junior high school classes.
- "Linguists... need to be more involved in the community itself,... working to influence... and be influenced by the attitudes of parents, students and teachers."
- There is a need to "start small." The authors recommend that work begin perhaps in one of the new Afrocentric private schools.
- "Research and experimentation on other means of teaching reading to working class speakers of AAVE, to others who need help with this essential skills" should be simultaneously investigated along with the use of dialect readers. "The idea," the authors contend, "is not to resurrect the issue of dialect readers as a cult or religion, but consider them as one of several possibilities to which linguists may be willing to contribute research time and effort as we become involved once more with educational issues."

Quoted with permission

Note

1. © Center for Applied Linguistics (www.cal.org). Revised: 3/28/97. For more information contact carolyn@cal.org. Reprinted with permission. Originally appeared in *Linguistics and Education* 7 (2), 107–128, 1995.

CONGRESSIONAL TESTIMONY

Submitted by William Labov, Professor of Linguistics at the University of Pennsylvania, Past President of the Linguistic Society of America, member of the National Academy of Science.
January 23, 1997

I am testifying today as a representative of an approach to the study of language that is called "sociolinguistics," a scientific study based on the recording and measurement of language as it is used in America today. I am now completing research supported by NSF and NEH that is mapping changes in the English language through all of North America, for both mainstream and minority communities. Since 1966, I have done a number of studies of language in the African American community, beginning with work in South Harlem for the Office of Education that was aimed at the question, "Are the language differences between black and white children responsible for reading failure in the inner city schools?"

The term "Ebonics," our main focus here, has been used to suggest that there is a language, or features of language, common to all people of African ancestry, whether they live in Africa, Brazil or the United States. Linguists who have published studies of the African American community do not use this term, but refer instead to African American Vernacular English, a dialect spoken by most residents of the inner cities. This African American Vernacular English shares most of its grammar and vocabulary with other dialects of English. But it is distinct in many ways, and it is more different from standard English than any other dialect spoken in continental North America. It is not simply slang, or grammatical mistakes, but a well-formed set of rules of pronunciation and grammar that is capable of conveying complex logic and reasoning.

Research in New York, Philadelphia, Washington, Florida, Chicago, Texas, Los Angeles, and San Francisco shows a remarkably uniform grammar spoken by African Americans who live and work primarily with other African Americans. Repeated studies by teams of black and white researchers show that about 60% of the African American residents of the inner city speak this dialect in its purist form at home and with intimate friends. Passive exposure to standard English – through the mass media or in school – has little effect upon the home language of children from highly segregated inner city areas. However, those African Americans who have had extensive face-to-face dealings with speakers of other dialects show a marked modification of their grammar.

In the first two decades of research, linguists were divided in their views of the origin of African American English, whether it was a Southern regional dialect descended from nonstandard English and Irish dialects, or the descendant of a Creole grammar similar to that spoken in the Caribbean. By 1980, a consensus seemed to have been reached, as expressed in the verdict of Judge Charles Joyner in the King trial in Ann Arbor: this variety of language showed the influence of the entire history of the African American people from slavery to modern times, and was gradually converging with other dialects.

However, research in the years that followed found that in many of its important features, African American Vernacular English was becoming not less, but more different from other dialects. Research on the language of ex-slaves showed that some of the most prominent features of the modern dialect were not present in the 19th century. It appears that the present-day form of African American English is not the inheritance of the period of slavery, but the creation of the second half of the 20th century.

An important aspect of the current situation is the strong social reaction against suggestions that the home language of African American children be used in the first steps of learning to read and write. The Oakland controversy is the fourth major reaction that I know of to proposals of this kind. Plans for programs to make the transition to standard English have been misunderstood as plans to teach the children to speak African American English, or Ebonics, and to prevent them from learning standard English. As a result, only one such program has been thoroughly tested in the schools, and even that program, though very successful in improving reading, was terminated because of objections to the use of any African American English in the classroom.

At the heart of the controversy, there are two major points of view taken by educators. One is that any recognition of a nonstandard language as a legitimate means of expression will only confuse children, and reinforce their tendency to use it instead of standard English. The other is that children learn most rapidly in their home language, and that they can benefit in both motivation and achievement by getting a head start in learning to read and write in this way. Both of these views are honestly held and deserve a fair hearing. But until now, only the first has been tried in the American public school system. The essence of the Oakland school board resolution is that the first method has not succeeded and that the second deserves a trial.

Research on reading shows that an essential step in learning to read is the mastery of the relation of sound to spelling. As linguists, we know that for most inner city African American children, this relation is different, and more complicated, than for speakers of other dialects. We have not yet been able to apply this knowledge to large-scale programs for the teaching of reading, but we hope that with the interest aroused by the Oakland School Board resolution, this will become possible in the near future.

Organizational Responses

POLICY STATEMENT OF THE TESOL BOARD ON AFRICAN AMERICAN VERNACULAR ENGLISH[1]

March 10, 1997

The Board of Directors of Teachers of English to Speakers of Other Languages (TESOL) is committed to strengthening the effective teaching and learning of English around the world. Its mission is to develop professional expertise and to foster effective communication in diverse settings while respecting individual language rights.

In accordance with its Policy on Language Varieties, October 1996, TESOL affirms that the variety of English known as African American Vernacular English, Black English, Ebonics and sometimes by other names, has been shown through research to be a rule-governed, linguistic system, with its own lexical, phonological, syntactic and discourse patterns and, thus, deserves pedagogical recognition.

The Board notes that effective educational programs recognize and value the linguistic systems that children bring to school. These programs use these linguistics systems as an aid and resource to facilitate the acquisition of Standard American English. Research and experience have shown that children learn best if teachers respect the home language and use it as a bridge in teaching the language of the school and wider society. Likewise, if the children's cultural and social backgrounds are valued, their self-respect and self-confidence are affirmed and new learning is facilitated.

TESOL thus advocates that teacher education include instruction in linguistics and in developing partnerships between the home and school.

Note
1. © Reprinted with permission.

POLICY STATEMENT OF THE AMERICAN ASSOCIATION FOR APPLIED LINGUISTICS (AAAL) ON THE APPLICATION OF DIALECT KNOWLEDGE TO EDUCATION

March 11, 1997

Resolution on the Application of Dialect Knowledge to Education

WHEREAS, The American Association for Applied Linguistics recognizes the legitimacy of African American language systems, variously referred to as African-American Vernacular English, Black English, or Ebonics, and their pedagogical importance in helping students acquire standard English;

WHEREAS, Public discussion of the Oakland School Board's decision on the legitimacy of Ebonics and its usefulness in teaching standard English demonstrates a lack of public awareness and understanding of the nature and naturalness of different varieties of language; and

WHEREAS, Students' competence in any dialect of English constitutes an important resource for learning standard English as an additional dialect;

THEREFORE BE IT RESOLVED at the general business meeting of the American Association for Applied Linguistics, convened on this 11th day of March, 1997:

(1) THAT, All students and teachers should learn scientifically-based information about linguistic diversity and examine the social, political, and educational consequences of differential treatment of dialects and their speakers;

(2) THAT, Teacher education should systematically incorporate information about language variation and its impact on classroom interaction and about ways of applying that knowledge to enhance the education of all teachers;

(3) THAT, Research should be undertaken to develop and test methods and materials for teaching about varieties of language and for learning standard English; and

(4) THAT, Members of the American Association for Applied Linguistics should seek ways and means to better communicate the theories and principles of the field to the general public on a continuing basis.

END

FOLLOW UP ACTIVITIES (posted on the AAAL home page: http://www.aaal.org)

Researchers and Educators Advocate Wider Understanding of Language Diversity

A group of nationally recognized leaders in education, linguistics, communication, and speech pathology called upon public school officials to take seriously the systematic differences among varieties of spoken and written English common in this country. Language differences play a critical role in instructional effectiveness, student learning, and educational assessment, according to Donna Christian, President of the Center for Applied Linguistics. These conclusions were reached at a Conference on language Diversity and Academic Achievement in the Education of African American Students in New York City on January 11 and 12, 1998. The conference was sponsored by national professional and research organizations. "The classroom is a communicative environment and most instruction and assessment involves the use of language," says Orlando Taylor, Dean of the Graduate School of Arts and Sciences at Howard University. "A disregard for language diversity can inhibit effective instruction and student learning and can result in inappropriate evaluation of student achievement," he continues.

For example, those attending the conference agreed that contrasts between standard English and some of the varieties of English spoken by African American students frequently lead to ineffective classroom instruction and mistakes in identifying predictable differences between language varieties as deficiencies in reading, writing, and speaking. This lack of understanding pairs with negative attitudes to foster low expectations that often impede academic achievement for the students involved. Researchers urged teacher education programs to give the nation's teachers accurate and practical information about language and dialect diversity to enhance their ability to teach students that come from a variety of language communities. They also described successful programs for training teachers and their students about how English varies in different geographical regions and social groups.

Attending the conference were teachers, school administrators, educational researchers, linguists, speech pathologists, communication scholars, professors, university deans, and representatives of the sponsoring organizations.

The conference was sponsored by the American Association for Applied Linguistics, the American Dialect Society, the American Speech-Language-Hearing Association, the Center for Applied Linguistics, the Council of the Great City Schools, Howard University's Graduate School of Arts and Sciences, the Linguistic Society of America, the National Alliance of Black School Educators, the National Black Association for Speech-Language and Hearing, the National Communication Association, the National Council of Teachers of English, the Office of Educational Research and Improvement at the U.S. Department of Education, and Teachers of English to Speakers of Other Languages.

CENTER FOR APPLIED LINGUISTICS (CAL) STATEMENT TO THE MEDIA ON EBONICS[1]

January 13, 1997

The Center for Applied Linguistics has played a key role in work on the various dialects of English. This work is part of our mission, which is to apply the research of the linguistic sciences to the educational, social and cultural issues of U.S. society.

In light of the recent wide-ranging discussion about Ebonics, or African American Vernacular English (AAVE), we have prepared a small packet of information on the use of dialects in U.S. society.

The Digest and the Minibib were developed through the Educational Resources Information Center (ERIC) database and network. ERIC is a valuable source for information on dialects. Summaries of journal articles as well as full texts of papers, curricula and other publications are to be found in this database that is funded by the U.S. Department of Education. We encourage you to search the database to get a fuller understanding of the ongoing issues inherent in the debate about this topic. Also included is a summary of an article on dialect readers by John and Angela Rickford of Stanford University, which includes information on some recent research conducted in the San Francisco area [Available in Linguists' Reactions section].

Two opinions about this debate are also included. Charles Fillmore, professor of Linguistics at University of California, Berkeley, takes a thoughtful look at the pedagogically relevant assumptions of the Oakland Unified School District's Ebonics Resolution [Available in Linguists' Reactions section]. And Carolyn Adger, a sociolinguist who has conducted research on AAVE in schools, comments on language policy and public knowledge, and she suggests the Ebonics debate provides an opportunity to improve language instruction for all students, not only those who speak a dialect other than standard English.

Finally, the recently approved resolution by the Linguistic Society of America which sets forth important language facts that bear on dialect programs is enclosed. The Society's Statement on Language Rights is also included because the resolution refers to it.

If you have questions about the enclosed materials or about this topic in general, please do not hesitate to contact Carolyn Adger or me at the Center.

Donna Christian

President

Note

1. © Center for Applied Linguistics (www.cal.org). Revised: 1/21/97. For more information contact carolyn@cal.org. Reprinted with permission.

CALIFORNIA ASSOCIATION FOR BILINGUAL EDUCATION (CABE) POSITION STATEMENT ON EBONICS

March 1997

(Prepared by Robert Berdan, Terrence G. Wiley, and Magaly Lavadenz)

This position statement by the California Association for Bilingual Education (CABE) addresses the current controversy regarding the status and role of Ebonics in education. As an organization committed to promoting equitable education and respect for speakers of all languages, CABE joins a host of other educational and professional associations by explicating its position on the Ebonics debate. Given the recent media barrage, misunderstanding, and hastily conceived proposed legislation, CABE believes that it is essential to clarify its position on the issue.

Historical Perspective
General Principles

- **CABE acknowledges and respects the cumulating of more than a quarter century of scientific research, the long-standing judgment of other professional associations, and the opinion of the federal courts establishing the structured and rule-governed legitimacy of Ebonics as a bona fide form of human communication.**

The legitimacy of Ebonics (variously called African American Vernacular English, Black English, Black Dialect, and African American Language) has long been recognized by many linguists (Bailey, 1965, 1969; Turner, 1949; Labov, 1970, 1972, 1982; Baugh, 1983; Dillard, 1972; Rickford, 1996; Roy, 1987; Smitherman, 1970, 1977; Williams, 1991), by professional organizations (Adger, 1996), and by the courts (Labov, 1982; Whiteman, 1980; Wright, 1980). In 1979, a major legal challenge (*Martin Luther King Jr. Elementary School Children vs. Ann Arbor Board of Education*) asserted that the differences between the language of African Americans

191

and the language of school were significant enough to warrant the recognition of Ebonics as a distinct variety of language. The suit was filed because, despite a district integration plan, African American children performed at a significantly lower level than their white peers. The plaintiffs argued that the school's failure to take into account the language differences of African American students was discriminatory, and the presiding judge concurred (Smitherman, 1981; Wiley, 1996).

- **CABE acknowledges the complex, both tragic and affirmative, history behind Ebonics; that the terms "language" and "dialect" have very different and confusing meanings in technical and popular discourse; and that linguists recognize that such distinctions are generally formed on social and political grounds, not on linguistic or historical characteristics.**

The perennial attacks on Ebonics as being a substandard dialect are based largely on ignorance of its history and richness as a distinct variety of language (Dandy, 1991; Williams, 1991). Although the majority of African Americans are native speakers of English, their linguistic history is related to their sociopolitical and economic history. That history is substantially different from that of many European-origin speakers of English and from that of speakers of other languages in the United States (Roy, 1987; Williams, 1975). Unlike most European-origin peoples who came to the United States either voluntarily or as political, religious, or economic refugees, the migration of most African-origin peoples was forced. During their enslavement, African Americans were denied access to English literacy through the imposition of compulsory ignorance laws (Weinberg, 1995). Despite these inhumanities, African Americans developed a unique, vital and creative language, strongly influenced by its West African antecedents (Asante, 1972, 1990; Bailey, 1965; Bailey, Mayor & Cukor-Avila; Dalby, 1969; Dillard, 1972; Roy, 1987). Spoken forms of language were ascribed a lower status than higher status written varieties of English (Dandy, 1991; Heath, 1983; Leacock, 1972; Kochman, 1986).

Linguistic and Cultural Perspectives

- **CABE recognizes that social institutions that value families and their impact on children have an affirmative obligation to demonstrate respect and appreciation for the communication of the home.**

In contemporary American society what is often characterized as "standard English" has a privileged status. Schools have an obligation to ensure all students from all linguistic backgrounds develop literacy and oral proficiency in standard English. However, the acquisition of standard English ought not lead to the eradication of the form of communication in the home language.

Students need to achieve productive competence in the grammar of standard English in order to achieve educational, social and economic mobility in this society. Nevertheless, the acquisition of standard English should be an additive process and need not reject or excise the dialect form of the family and peers. Thus, schools should seek to build on students' knowledge of Ebonics.

- **CABE acknowledges that the relationships among race, ethnicity, and language are complex and varied, both for individuals and for communities. However, there is close identification of Ebonics with broad segments of the African American community. Derogatory characterizations as "bad," "broken," "ignorant," or "ungrammatical" in the popular press or in casual conversation strain the social fabric both in schools and in the broader society.**

Language prejudice is related to other forms of intolerance and frequently becomes a surrogate for them. In a society as racially, ethnically, and linguistically diverse as ours, children and adults need to learn more about the richness of their own languages and varieties of languages. (Brooks, 1985; Dandy, 1991; Heath, 1983; Wiley, 1996; Wolfram, 1994). Teachers have an obligation to model for their students the respect and appreciation for the linguistic diversity of the larger society as they foster in their students appreciation for the conventions of standard English. Implicit and explicit educational practices should be examined to ensure that discriminatory treatment does not result in stigmatization and inappropriate educational treatment.

- **CABE affirms the responsibility of schools to take appropriate action to overcome language barriers that impede equal participation by its students in its instructional programs set forth by the Equal Educational Opportunities Act of 1974. This action can be further expanded by the *Lau v. Nichols* and *ML King, Jr. Elementary School v. Ann Arbor Board of Education* (1979) which obligated schools to recognize and accommodate language differences that would otherwise result in meaningless inequitable education.**

Teachers and schools have an obligation to develop an instructional environment where all students, including speakers of Ebonics, are encouraged to participate freely and actively without harassment or ridicule for the way they speak. In classroom discourse, and particularly when the focus of instruction is not on language, effective teachers focus first and positively on the content of what students say, particularly on their logic, creativity, and contribution to the communication.

Control of the conventions of standard English develops over extended time. Schools facilitate that development by engaging students in meaningful literacy experiences, by engaging them in increasingly complex discourse, and by providing them with meaningful contexts that presuppose standard English. In all of these experiences students gain more from recognition for their evolving language than from demeaning their home language.

English Literacy and Ebonics

- **CABE concludes that in contemporary American society literacy is a basic educational right. Meaningful literacy experiences must be accessible to children from all linguistic backgrounds as early in their educational experience as possible. English literacy is an important tool and context for the development of standard English.**

Whatever the language or dialect that students bring to school, we consider literacy instruction to be a basic human right, and English literacy instruction to be requisite to full social, economic, and political participation in the United States. For educators, this means that literacy instruction cannot be made contingent on a child's ability to conform to school-determined languages and dialects. Pronunciation differences in reading by African American students should not be considered as reading errors. Therefore, children's access to meaningful literacy instruction must not be withheld until such time as they become standard speakers of English. Moreover, literacy involves more than just grammar and pronunciation. Multicultural literacy involves awareness of a broad range of discourse styles and genres and their appropriate uses in specific social contexts.

- **CABE concludes that the recent emphasis on phonics in English literacy instruction must be sensitive to the systematic differences between Ebonics and standard English.**

Initial literacy instruction accepts and builds upon, without diminishing or depreciating, the language skills that children bring to school. At the same time the materials utilized in reading instruction should be authentic and should realistically reflect students' cultural and linguistic backgrounds. Schools can affirm linguistic and cultural diversity by demonstrating respect for the ways in which children, families and their communities communicate.

Ebonics and Language Diversity in the Broader Curriculum

- **CABE affirms the need to link an understanding of and appreciation for language diversity to multicultural education and anti-racist education.**

Linguistic diversity is an important and enduring characteristic of contemporary America, of its history, and of the world around us. Until recently, the curriculum has been silent on issues of linguistic diversity and its relationship to race and racism, ethnicity and ethnocentrism, and to issues of power, prestige and social dominance. These are all legitimate topics on which the curriculum has too long been silent. Students deserve honest and open discussion of these topics across the curriculum.

Implications for Teacher Training

- **CABE recommends that all teachers in California need expertise and sensitivity to teach positively and productively in classrooms with students from diverse linguistic backgrounds and with differing levels of English proficiency.**

It is essential that teachers possess the knowledge necessary to do their job. Teachers of English who deal with speakers of Ebonics need to be trained so that they know enough about standard English and Ebonics to teach systematically those forms of standard English that are needed by their students. Teaching approaches, methods and techniques need to be developed and implemented that go beyond the techniques employed to teach those who already know the standard dialect and address the students who possess the structurally different forms of Black English (Roy, 1987).

Most teachers experience in their classrooms at least some students from linguistic backgrounds that differ substantially from their own experience. All teachers are encouraged to develop their language abilities as broadly as possible, but it is particularly important that teachers develop the ability to understand and respond appropriately to the diverse forms of English spoken by students in California schools.

Schools and teacher training institutions must select master teachers who will seek to create positive and supportive learning environments for students of all linguistic backgrounds. Teachers with direct responsibility for the development of literacy skills need a working knowledge of Ebonics, its sound system and its unique grammatical characteristics.

Recommended Readings on Ebonics

Scholarly References and News Titles

Compiled by
WAYNE E. WRIGHT

Scholarly References

Adger, C. (1994) *Enhancing the Delivery of Services to Black Special Education Students from Non-standard English Backgrounds. Final report*. University of Maryland, Institute for the Study of Exceptional Children and Youth. (ERIC Document No. ED 370 377).

Adger, C. (1995) *Issues and Implications of English Dialects for TESOL*. Washington, DC: Center for Applied Linguistics.

Adger, C., Christian, D. and Taylor, O. (1999) *Making the Connection: Language and Academic Achievement Among African American Students*. Washington, DC and McHenry, IL: Center for Applied Linguistics and Delta Systems, Inc.

Adger, C., Wolfram, W. and Detwyler, J. (1993a) Language differences: A new approach for special educators. *Teaching Exceptional Children* 26 (1), 44–47.

Adger, C., Wolfram, W., Detwyler, J. and Harry, B. (1993b) Confronting dialect minority issues in special education: Reactive and proactive perspectives. In *Proceedings of the Third National Research Symposium on Limited English Proficient Student Issues: Focus on Middle and High School Issues* (Vol. 2 pp. 737–762). US Department of Education, Office of Bilingual Education and Minority Languages Affairs. (ERIC Document No. ED 356 673.)

Asante, M.K. (ed.) (1972) *Language, Communication and Rhetoric in Black America*. New York: Harper & Row.

Asante, M.K. (1990) African elements in African American English. In J.E. Holloway (ed.) *Africanisms in American Culture*. Bloomington, IN: Indiana University Press.

Atlatis, J.E. and Tan, A.H. (eds) (2001) *Georgetown University Round Table on Languages and Linguistics 1999: Language in our Time: Bilingual Education and Official English, Ebonics and Standard English, Immigration and the Unz Initiative*. Washington, DC: Georgetown University Press.

Attinasi, J.J. (1994) Racism, language variety, and urban U.S. minorities: Issues in bilingualism and bidialectism. In S. Gregory and R. Sanjek (eds) *Race* (pp. 320–347). New Brunswick, NJ: Rutgers University Press.

Bailey, B.L. (1965) Toward a new perspective in Negro English dialectology. *American Speech* 40 (3), 170–177.

Bailey, B.L. (1969) Language and communicative styles of Afro-American children in the United States. *The Florida FL Reporter* Spring/Summer, 46, 153.

Bailey, G., Maynor, N. and Cukor-Avila, P. (eds) (1991) *The Emergence of Black English*. Amsterdam & Philadelphia: John Benjamins.

Baldwin, J. (1979) If Black English isn't a language, then tell me, what is? *The New York Times* July 29.

Baratz, J. and Shuy, R. (eds) (1969) *Teaching Black Children to Read*. Washington, DC: Center for Applied Linguistics.

Baratz, J. (1970) Educational considerations for teaching Standard English to Negro children. In R.W. Fasold and R.W. Shuy (eds) *Teaching Standard English in the Inner City* (pp. 20–40). Washington, DC: The Center for Applied Linguistics.

Baugh, J. (1983) *Black Street Speech: Its History, Structure and Survival*. Austin: University of Texas Press.

Baugh, J. (1995) The law, linguistics and education: Educational reform for African American language minority students. *Linguistics and Education* 7, 87–105.

Baugh, J. (1997) What's in a name? That by which we call the linguistic consequences of the African slave trade. *The Quarterly of the National Writing Project* 19 (9).

Baugh, J. (1998) Linguistics, education, and the law: Educational reform for African American language minority students. In S. Mufwene *et al.* (eds) *African American English: History, Structure, and Usage*. London: Routledge.

Baugh, J. (1999) *Out of the Mouths of Slaves: African American Language and Educational Malpractice*. Austin, TX: University of Texas Press.

Baugh, J. and Hymes, D. (2000) *Beyond Ebonics: Linguistic Pride and Racial Prejudice*. Oxford, UK: Oxford University Press.

Berdan, R. (1980) Knowledge into practice: Delivering research to teachers. In M.E. White (ed.) *Reactions to Ann Arbor: Vernacular Black English and Education*. Washington, DC: Center for Applied Linguistics.

Blackshire-Belay, A.C. (1996) The location of Ebonics within the framework of the Africological paradigm. *Journal of Black Studies* 27, 5–23.

Brooks, C.K. (ed.) (1985) *Tapping Potentials: English and Language Arts for the Black Learner*. Urbana, IL: National Council of Teachers of English.

Christian, D. (1997) *Vernacular Dialects and Standard American English in the Classroom*. (ERIC Minibib). Washington, DC: ERIC Clearinghouse on Languages and Linguistics.

Crawford, C. (ed.) (2001) *Ebonics and Language Education*. New York: Sankofa World Publishers.

Dalby, D. (1969) *Black through White: Patterns of Communication in Africa in the World*. Bloomington, IN: Indiana University Press.

Dalby, D. (1972) The African element in American English. In T. Kochman (ed.) *Rappin' and Stylin' Out: Communication in Urban Black America*. Chicago: University of Illinois Press.

Dandy, E.B. (1991) *Black Communications: Breaking Down the Barriers*. Chicago: African American Images.

De Franz, A. (1994) Coming to cultural and linguistic awakening: An African and African American educational vision. In J. Frederickson (ed.) *Reclaiming Our*

Voices: Bilingual Education Critical Pedagogy and Praxis. Ontario, CA: California Association for Bilingual Education.

Delpit, L. and Dowdy, J.K. (eds) (2001) *The Skin that We Speak: Thoughts on Language and Culture in the Classroom*. New York: New Press.

Dillard, J.L. (1972) *Black English: Its History and Usage in the United States*. New York: Vintage Books.

Dillard, J.L. (1977) *Lexicon of Black English*. New York: The Seabury Press.

Fanon, E. (1967) *The Negro and Language – Black Skin, White Masks*. New York: Grove Press Inc.

Fasold, R.W. and Wolfram, W. (1970) Some linguistic features of Negro dialect. In R.W. Fasold and R.W. Shuy (eds) *Teaching Standard English in the Inner City* (pp. 41–86). Washington, DC: The Center for Applied Linguistics.

Gadsden, V.L. and Wagner, D.A. (eds) (1995) *Literacy among African-American Youth: Issues in Learning, Teaching, and Schooling*. Cresskill, NJ: Hampton Press.

Harris, J.K. (2003) *Pan-African Language Systems: Ebonics and African Oral Heritage*. London: Karnak House.

Harris, J.L., Kamhi, A.G. *et al.* (eds) (2001) *Literacy in African American Communities*. Mahwah, NJ: Lawrence Erlbaum.

Harrison, J.A. (1984) Negro English. *Anglia* 7, 232–279.

Heath, S.B. (1983) *Ways with Words. Language, Life, and Work in Communities and Classrooms*. Cambridge: Cambridge University Press.

Heynick, F. (1997) *The Ebonics Controversy: Exploring the Roots of an African American Dialect*. New York: Birch Lane.

Hoover, M.R. (1987) Bias in reading tests for Black language speakers: A sociolinguistic perspective. *Negro Educational Review* 38 (2–3), 81–98.

Illich, I. (1979) Vernacular values and education. *Teacher's College Record* 81 (1), 31–75.

Key, M., Kollman, L. and Smith, E. (1971) Features of child Black English. In W. Mackey and T. Anderson (eds) *Bilingualism in Early Childhood*. MA: Newbury House.

Kochman, T. (ed.) (1972) *Rapping' and Stylin' Out. Communication in Urban Black America*. Urbana, IL: University of Illinois Press.

Kochman, T. (1986) *Black and White Styles in Conflict*. Chicago: The University of Chicago Press.

Labov, W. (1970) *The Study of Nonstandard English*. Champaign, IL: National Council of Teachers of English.

Labov, W. (1972) *Language in the Inner City: Studies in the Black English Vernacular*. Philadelphia: University of Pennsylvania Press.

Labov, W. (1982) Objectivity and commitment in linguistic science: The case of the Black English trial in Ann Arbor. *Language and Society* 11, 165–201.

Leacock, E.B. (1972) Abstract versus concrete speech: A false dichotomy. In C.B. Cazden, V.P. John and D. Hymes (eds) *Functions of Language in the Classroom* (pp. 111–134). Prospect Heights, IL: Waveland Press.

Lippi-Green, R. (1994) Accent, standard language ideology, and discriminatory pretext in courts. *Language in Society* 23, 163–198.

Lippi-Green, R. (1997) *English with an Accent: Language, Ideology, and Discrimination in the United States*. London: Routledge.

Loyd, B.H. and Williams, T.E. (1982) *Attractiveness of "Black English" foils: An Examination of a Potential Source of Item Bias*. Paper presented at the American Educational Research Association, New York (Eric Document No. ED222581).

Major, C. (1970) *Dictionary of Afro-American Slang*. New York: International Publishers.

Milroy, J. and Milroy, L. (1985) *Authority in Language: Investigating Language Prescription and Standardization*. London: Routledge and Kegan Paul.

Mufwene, S.S., Rickford, J.R., Bailey, G. and Baugh, J. (eds) (1988) *The Structure of African American Vernacular English*. New York: Routledge.

Pandey, A. (2000) TOEFL to the test: Are monodialectal AAL-speakers similar to ESL students? *World Englishes* 19 (1), 89–106.

Perry, T. and Delpit, L. (ed.) (1998) *The Real Ebonics Debate*. Boston, MA: Beacon Press.

Piestrup, A.M. (1973) Black Dialect interference and accommodation of reading instruction in first grade. *Monographs of the Language Behavior Research Laboratory* 4. Berkeley: University of California.

Quay, L.C. (1971) Language, dialect, reinforcement, and the intelligence-test performance of Negro children. *Child Development* 42, 5–15.

Quay, L.C. (1972) Negro dialect and Binet performance in severely disadvantaged Black four-year-olds. *Child Development* 43, 245–230.

Quay, L.C. (1974) Language, dialect, age, and intelligence-test performance in disadvantaged Black children. *Child Development* 45, 463–468.

Richardson, E. (1998) The anti-Ebonics movement: 'Standard English-only.' *Journal of English Linguistics* 26 (2).

Rickford, J.R. (1977) The question of prior creolization in Black English. In A. Valdman (ed.) *Pidgin and Creole Linguistics* (pp. 190–221). Bloomington: Indiana University Press.

Rickford, J.R. (1986) Social contact and linguistic diffusion: Hiberno English and new world Black English. *Language* 62, 245–90.

Rickford, J.R. (1992) Grammatical variation and divergence in Vernacular Black English. In M. Gerritsen and D. Stein (eds) *Internal and External Factors in Syntactic Change* (pp. 175–200). Berlin: Mouton.

Rickford, J.R. (1996) Ebonics succeeds where traditional methods do not. *San Jose Mercury News* December 26, 8B.

Rickford, J. (1996) Regional and social variation. In S.L. McKay and N. Hornberger (eds) *Social Linguistics and Language Teaching* (pp. 151–194). Cambridge, UK: Cambridge University Press.

Rickford, J.R. (1997a) Prior creolization of AAVE? Sociohistorical and textual evidence from the 17th and 18th centuries. *Journal of Sociolinguistics* 1 (3), 315–336.

Rickford, J.R. (1997b) Unequal partnership: Sociolinguistics and the African American speech community. *Language in Society* 26 (2), 161–197.

Rickford, J. (1997c) Suite for Ebony and phonics. *Discover Magazine*.

Rickford, J.R. (1997d) Ebonics and education: Lessons from the Caribbean, Europe and the USA. Paper presented at the national symposium, *What is the Relationship of Ebonics to the Education of Black Americans?* Held at Medgar Evers College, City University of New York, Brooklyn, NY, January 25, 1997.

Roy, J.D. (1987) The linguistic and sociolinguistic position of Black English and the issue of bidialectism in education. In P. Homel, M. Palij and D. Aaronson (eds) *Childhood Bilingualism: Aspects of Linguistic, Cognitive, and Social Development* (pp. 231–242). Mahwah, NJ: Lawrence Erlbaum Associates.

Simons, H.D. and Johnson K.R. (1974) Black English syntax and reading interference. *Research in the Teaching of English* 8, 339–358.

Smith, E.A. (1978) The Retention of the phonological, phonemic, and morphophonemic features of Africa in Afro-American Ebonics. *Department of Linguistics Seminar Papers Series No. 43.* Fullerton, CA: California State University.

Smith, E.A. (1992) African American language behavior: A world of difference. In E.H. Dryer (ed.) *Claremont Reading Conference* (pp. 39–53). Pomona: Claremont College.

Smith, E.A. (1993) The black child in the schools: Ebonics and its implications for the transformation of American education. In A. Darder (ed.) *Bicultural Studies in Education: The Struggle for Educational Justice* (pp. 58–76). Claremont, CA: Claremont Graduate School, Institute for Education in Transformation.

Smith, E.A. (1994) *The Historical Development of African American Language.* Los Angeles, CA: Watts College Press.

Smith, E.A. (1995) Bilingualism and the African American child. In M.B. Joshua-Shearer, B.E. Pugh and B.A. Schaudt (eds) *Reading: The Blending of Theory and Practice* (pp. 83–95). Bakersfield, CA: California State University.

Smith, E.A. (1997) What is Black English? What is Ebonics? *Rethinking Schools* Fall.

Smitherman, G. (1975) *Black Language and Culture: Sounds of Soul.* New York: Harper & Row.

Smitherman, G. (1981a) What go round come round: King in perspective. *Harvard Educational Review* February, 40–56.

Smitherman, G. (ed.) (1981b) Black English and the education of Black children and youth. In *Proceedings of the National Invitational Symposium on the King decision.* Detroit, MI: Center for Black Studies, Wayne State.

Smitherman, G. (1992) African Americans and English only. *Language Problems and Language Planning* 16, 235–248.

Smitherman, G. (1994) *Black Talk.* Boston: Houghton Mifflin.

Smitherman, G. (1995) Students' right to their own language: A retrospective. *English Journal* 84 (1).

Smitherman, G. (1998) Ebonics, King, and Oakland: Some folks don't believe fat meat is greasy. *Journal of English Linguistics* June (special issue on Ebonics).

Smitherman, G. (1999) African Americans, Ebonics, and U.S. language planning-policy. In L. Limage (ed.) *Comparative Perspectives on Language and Literacy.* Dakar, Senegal: UNESCO.

Smitherman, G. (2000a) *Talkin that Talk: Language, Culture and Education in African America.* New York: Routledge.

Smitherman, G. (2000b) *Black Talk: Words and Phrases from the Hood to the Amen Corner* (rev. ed.). New York: Houghton Mifflin.

Smitherman, G. (2001) A commentary on Ebonics: From a ghetto lady turned critical linguist. In C. Crawford (ed.) *Ebonics and Language Education.* New York: Sankofa World Publishers.

Smitherman, G. (2001) Leroy, Big D, and Big Daddy speakin Ebonics on the internet. *American Language Review* March/April.

Turner, L.D. (1974) *Africanisms in the Gullah Dialect*. Ann Arbor, MI: The University of Michigan Press.

Welmers, W.E. (1973) *African Language Structures*. Berkeley, CA: University of California Press.

Whiteman, M.E. (ed.) (1980) Reactions to Ann Arbor. *Vernacular Black English and Education*. Washington, DC: Center for Applied Linguistics.

Wiener, F.D. (1983) Measuring language competency in speakers of Black American English. *Journal of Speech and Hearing Disorders* 48 (1), 76–84.

Wiley, T.G. (1996) The case of African American language. In T.G. Wiley (ed.) *Literacy and Language Diversity in the United States* (pp. 125–132). Washington, DC and McHenry, IL: Center for Applied Linguistics and Delta Systems.

Williams, R.L. (1972) *The BITCH-100: A Culture-Specific Test*. Paper presented at the American Psychological Association, Honolulu, HI (Eric Document No. ED070799).

Williams, R. (1975) *Ebonics. The True Language of Black folks*. St. Louis: Robert Williams and Associates.

Wolfram, W. (1969) *A Linguistic Description of Detroit Negro Speech*. Washington, DC: Center for Applied Linguistics.

Wolfram, W., Adger, C.T. and Christian, D. (1998) *Dialects in Schools and Communities*. Mahwah, NJ: Erlbaum.

Wolfram, W. and Fasold, R.W. (1974) *The Study of Social Dialects in American English*. Englewood Cliffs, NJ: Prentice-Hall.

Wolfram, W. and Schilling-Estes, N. (1998) *American English*. Oxford, UK: Blackwell.

News Titles 1996–2003

The following newspaper articles can be accessed online in the News Archives of the Language Policy Research Unit at http://www.language-policy.org

Clarence Page, Ebonics: Linguistic Apartheid? The uses and abuses of 'Black' English. *Chicago Tribune* December 25, 1996.

The Ebonics Resolution needs a major overhaul. *San Francisco Chronicle* January 2, 1997.

Educators defend use of Ebonics. *Los Angeles Times* January 3, 1997.

Kevin Weston, The state of Ebonics and the relevance of a school's curriculum. *Los Angeles Times* January 5, 1997.

Lori Olszewski, Slight rewriting of Ebonics policy sought in Oakland. *San Francisco Chronicle* January 8, 1997.

Lori Olszewski, Teacher's union to address Ebonics; strike leader skeptical of Oakland plan. *San Francisco Chronicle* January 11, 1997.

Joan Ryan, Unfamiliar cadences from a familiar voice. *San Francisco Chronicle* January 12, 1997.

Language of a community is determined culturally. *Florida Times Union (Jacksonville)* January 13, 1997.

Ellen Warren and Janita Poe, Ebonics; doing what it takes to communicate. *Chicago Tribune* January 14, 1997.

Marc Lacey, U.S. Senate panel grills officials on Ebonics policy. *Los Angeles Times* January 24, 1997.

Robert B. Gunnison, GOP Senator seeks to punish state's Ebonics schools; bill would bar use of funds for teaching. *San Francisco Chronicle* January 29, 1997.

Lucia Herndon, Farewell to Ebonics – let's focus on Standard English. *Philadelphia Inquirer* June 1, 1997.

Cristy DeAraujo, For real doe, this is fab talk. Slang is alive with poetry, possibilities and humor. *Providence Journal-Bulletin (Rhode Island)* June 16, 1997.

Lori Olszewski, Oakland parent calls for boycott of schools; Ebonics champion says blacks aren't being taught. *Chronicle East Bay Bureau, The San Francisco Chronicle* June 26, 1997.

Lori Olszewski, Mixed views on school boycott call; Oakland parents are reluctant to pull kids. *Chronicle East Bay Bureau, The San Francisco Chronicle* June 27, 1997.

Lori Olszewski, Black Studies Dept. sought in Oakland; Supporters crowd district headquarters. *The San Francisco Chronicle* July 17, 1997.

Ebonics' chief backer leaves school post. *Dayton Daily News (Ohio)* August 7, 1997.

Ebonics' defender resigns from district. *Milwaukee Journal Sentinel (Wisconsin)* August 7, 1997.

Official who advocated Black English resigns. *The Record (Bergen County, NJ)* August 7, 1997.

Alice Ann Love, Black psychologists hear defense of Ebonics. *The Commercial Appeal (Memphis, TN)* August 10, 1997.

Ebonics founder defends its linguistic value. *Charleston Gazette (West Virginia)* August 11, 1997.

To heck with Ebonics; Learn English. *News & Record (Greensboro, NC)* August 16, 1997.

Fractured Lingua Franca. *AdWeeK, Southwest Edition* August 18, 1997.

Ebonics is absurd, degrading. *The Advocate (Baton Rouge, LA)* August 25, 1997.

Nancy Trejos, Integration pioneer plans school for Blacks. *The Record (Bergen County, NJ)* November 24, 1997.

Ebonics hinders learning standard English. *Copley News Service* December 20, 1997.

Joseph H. Brown, Ebonics folly still good for laughs. *The Tampa Tribune (Florida)* December 21, 1997.

Michele Lynche, Deciphering Ebonics can be a daunting task. *St. Petersburg Times (Florida)* January 21, 1998.

Mike Toner, White-black vernacular gap widening; Linguists warn of 'bad omen' for American society. *The Atlanta Journal and Constitution* February 15, 1998.

Diane Loupe, School Watch; Teacher tells how to use black English. *The Atlanta Journal and Constitution* March 12, 1998.

Maryam Tanhaee, Ebonics: The sequel. *The Commercial Appeal (Memphis, TN)* April 15, 1998.

Rene Sanchez, After Ebonics controversy, Oakland seeks viable lesson plan. *Washington Post* April 19, 1998.

Nick Chiles, Talk of success with Ebonics; Class posts higher test scores. *Austin American-Statesman (Texas)* June 14, 1998.

The withering ridicule and misperceptions of Oakland's teaching strategy have come and gone. Now comes word and evidence that this language program may actually work. *The Post-Standard (Syracuse, NY)* June 18, 1998.

Stefani Carter, Ebonics handicap getting in the way. *The Washington Times* August 1, 1998.

Joan Stroer, Experts backing Ebonics. *Florida Times-Union (Jacksonville, FL)* October 13, 1998.

Rene A. Guzman, Switch lit Our Lady of the Lake festival explores bilingual poetry. *San Antonio Express-News (Texas)* November 4, 1998.

Jules Wagman, From 'Beowulf' to Black English: It's all healthy. *San Antonio Express-News (Texas)* January 3, 1999.

Lori Olszewski, Oakland schools to hold teach-in. *The San Francisco Chronicle* January, 8, 1999.

Thomas Sowell, Politics hurts public schools. *The Times Union (Albany, NY)* January 16, 1999.

Talking Ebonics. *Wisconsin State Journal (Madison, WI)* March 2, 1999.

Phil Brinkman, Exploring the world of Ebonics; Conference examines the use of Black dialect at home, school, and the workplace. *Wisconsin State Journal (Madison, WI)* March 5, 1999.

Howie Carr, Lawrence rep has invented new language. *The Boston Herald* May 5, 1999.

Wayne State University offers Ebonics course. *The Associated Press State & Local Wire* January 12, 2000.

Michelle Locke, Blackboard case raises bias questions. *Deseret News (Salt Lake City)* February 13, 2000.

City can't erase blackboard issue. *Telegraph Herald (Dubuque, IA)* February 14, 2000.

Debra J. Saunders, A tree grows in Oakland. *The San Francisco Chronicle* March 31, 2000.

Mayor's taunt at Bush's 'Ebonics'. *The San Francisco Chronicle* April 4, 2001.

Venise Wagner, Coming correct on Black English; Misperceptions about African American speech challenged. *The San Francisco Examiner* April 18, 2000.

Oakland paving terrorist streets. *Alameda Times-Star (Alameda, CA)* March 24, 2002.

Wolfgang Saxon, W.A. Stewart, Linguist, 71; Studied Ebonics. *The New York Times* April 10, 2002.

William A. Stewart; Proponent of Ebonics. *The Washington Post* April 14, 2002.

The roots of 'Ebonics'. *The Herald (Rock Hill, SC)* May 11, 2002.

Sean Gonsalves, Reminder of the power of words. *The Seattle Post-Intelligencer* June 11, 2002.

Stacy Day, Library to focus on black issues; Diversity of WWII force to be discussed. *Times-Picayune (New Orleans, LA)* June 20, 2002.

Nicholas Stix, Students hooked on 'Ebonics' are being groomed for failure. *Insight on the News* June 24, 2002.

Chauncey Mabe, Moving words; Evolution of languages argues for their equal status, writer says. *Charleston Gazette (West Virginia)* August 18, 2002.

Nothing wrong with Wagstaff's grammar. *The Herald-Sun (Durham, NC)* January 3, 2003.

Barbara Doyle, No to Ebonics. *The Herald-Sun (Durham, NC)* January 8, 2003.

Graham Marlette, 'Ebonics' and 'moronics'. *The Herald-Sun (Durham, NC)* January 9, 2003.

Amy Pyle, Boudreaux tries to win support for Ebonics plan. *Los Angeles Times* January 31, 2003.

Carolina Peacemaker, Linguist wins grant to advance study of Black speech. May 8, 2003.

Gloria Decamps. Why white American would rather learn Spanish than Ebonics. *Village Voice (New York, NY)* June 10, 2003.

Clarence Page, Parents can learn from immigrant success. *Newsday (New York)* September 9, 2003.